The Giant Book of Theme Patterns

Written by Jean Stangl
Illustrated by Walt Shelly

Fearon Teacher Aids
Simon & Schuster Education Group

Copyeditor: Kristin Eclov
Illustration and Design: Walt Shelly

ISBN 0-8224-6756-9

Printed in the United States of America

1.9 8 7 6 5 4 3 2 1

Contents

Introduction

Here's a teacher resource filled with just the right pattern for every occasion of the school year. This all-in-one book follows the school calendar and includes patterns for holidays, musical instruments, dinosaurs, the seasons, and other important study units. Use this resource to help bring a wider awareness of celebrations and stories to your classroom. There is also a time-saving index for quick reference.

The Giant Book of Theme Patterns will be of great help to teachers, but church, youth, and community leaders, librarians, parents, and children of all ages will find it a useful, one-of-a-kind resource, too.

Most of the patterns consist of simple outlines that can be used individually or combined with other patterns. You will find multiple uses for the patterns in a variety of art projects, including cutting, painting, coloring, and tracing. Use the patterns to make cardboard templates for children to trace and for creating bulletin boards, mobiles, room decorations, visual aids, flannelgraph figures, and posters. Duplicate the pages for teaching tools and games, too.

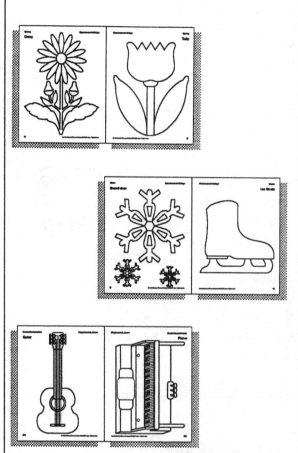

For young children, use the pictures for identification, discovering pairs (mittens, boots, skates), and seriating (trees, valentines, shamrocks). The patterns in the storytime section can be traced onto felt and used for board stories or attached to tongue depressors for stick puppets. Cut out the patterns and glue the shapes to cardboard. The story characters, community workers, and animals could be placed in the classroom dollhouse or block area to stimulate creative play.

You will discover many uses for the food pictures, including categorizing the foods into groups, using the patterns to study nutrition, helping students recognize foods, and learn about gardening. Try tracing and cutting out food items from colored construction paper, laminate, and then use the food shapes in your grocery-store unit. If you price the items, you'll have added a fun math activity, too. For additional teaching ideas, see *Teaching Units for the Giant Book of Theme Patterns* (a companion to this title, also published by Fearon Teacher Aids).

The table of contents enables you to quickly find patterns relating to the months, seasons, celebrations, and other general teaching units. Check the index for a complete listing of the 400+ patterns included in this text.

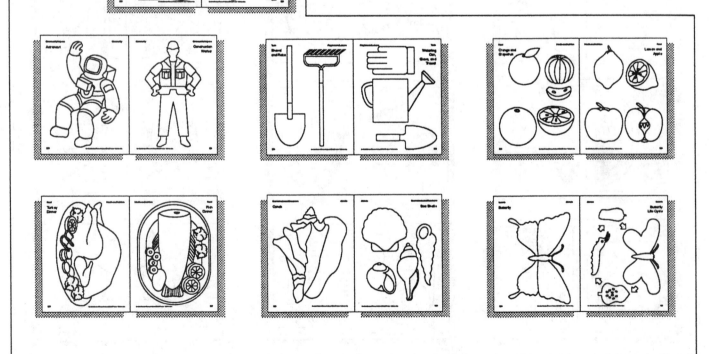

Acorn and
Oak Leaf

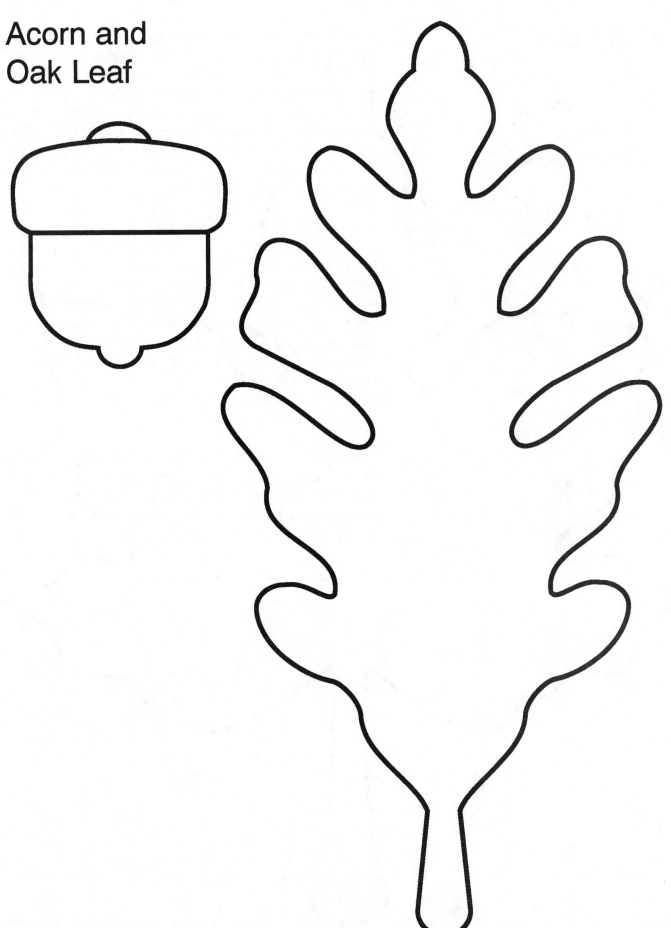

Maple Leaf

Sycamore Leaf

Pinecone

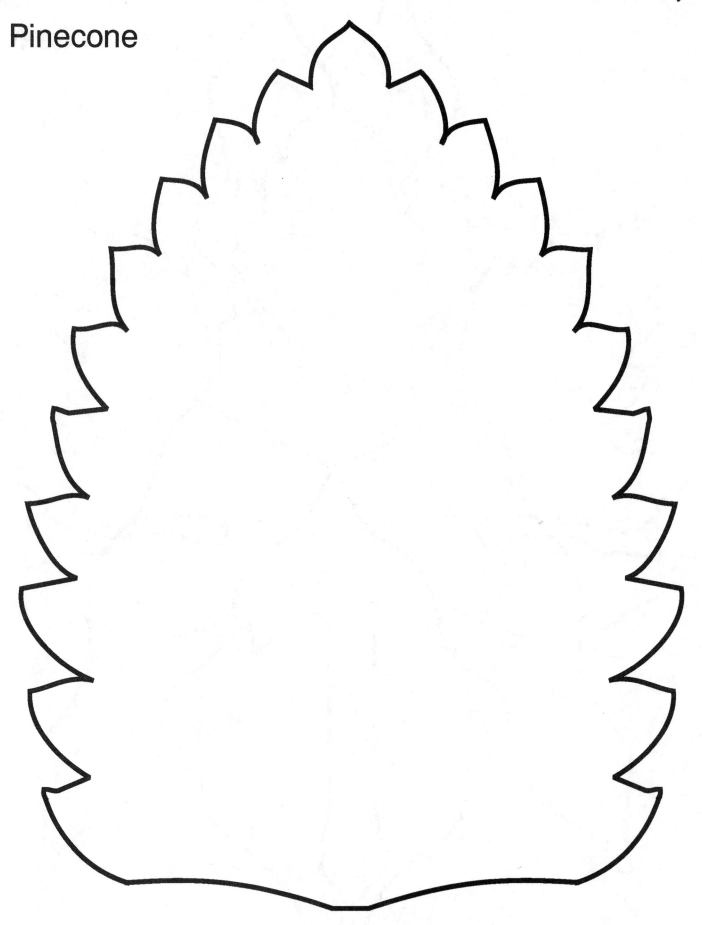

The Giant Book of Theme Patterns © 1993 Fearon Teacher Aids

Corn

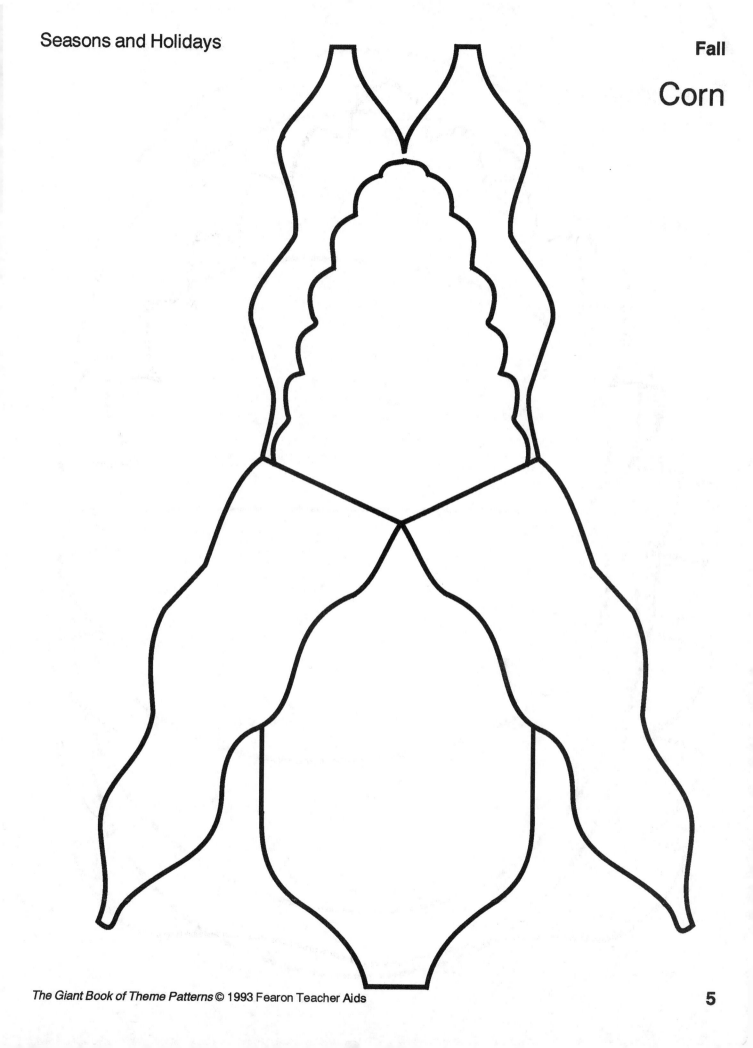

Pumpkin

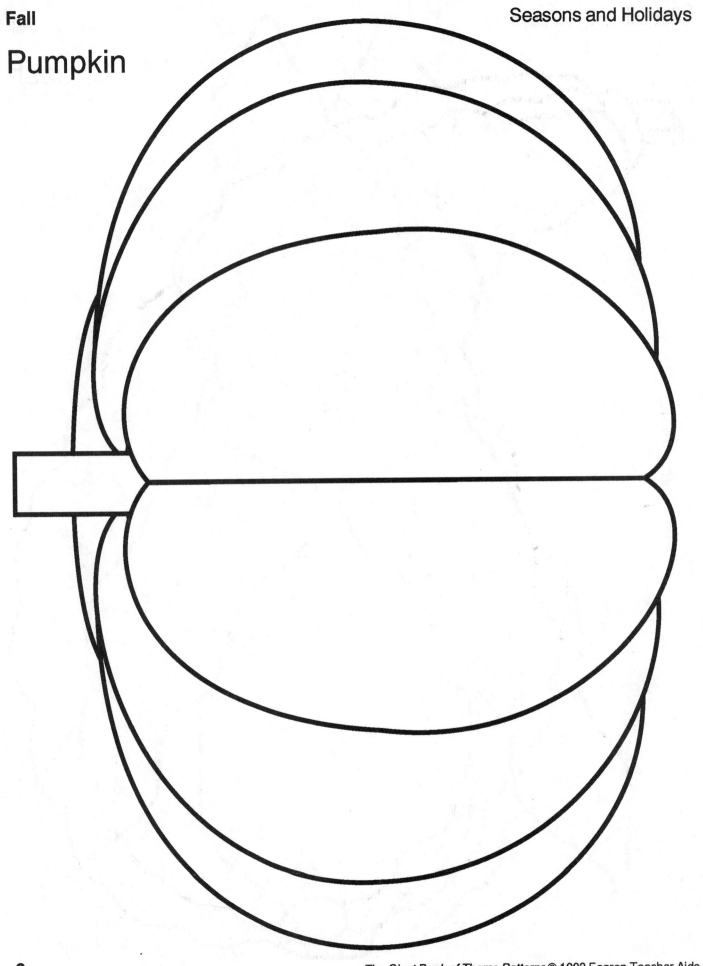

Squash

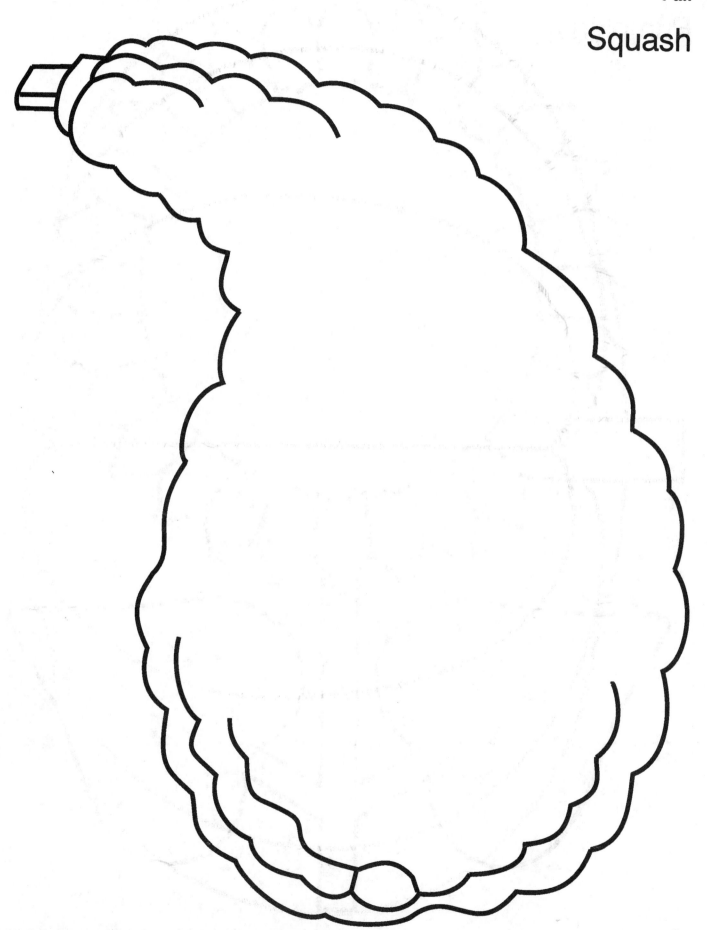

Sunflower

Snow Person

Sled

Winter Tree

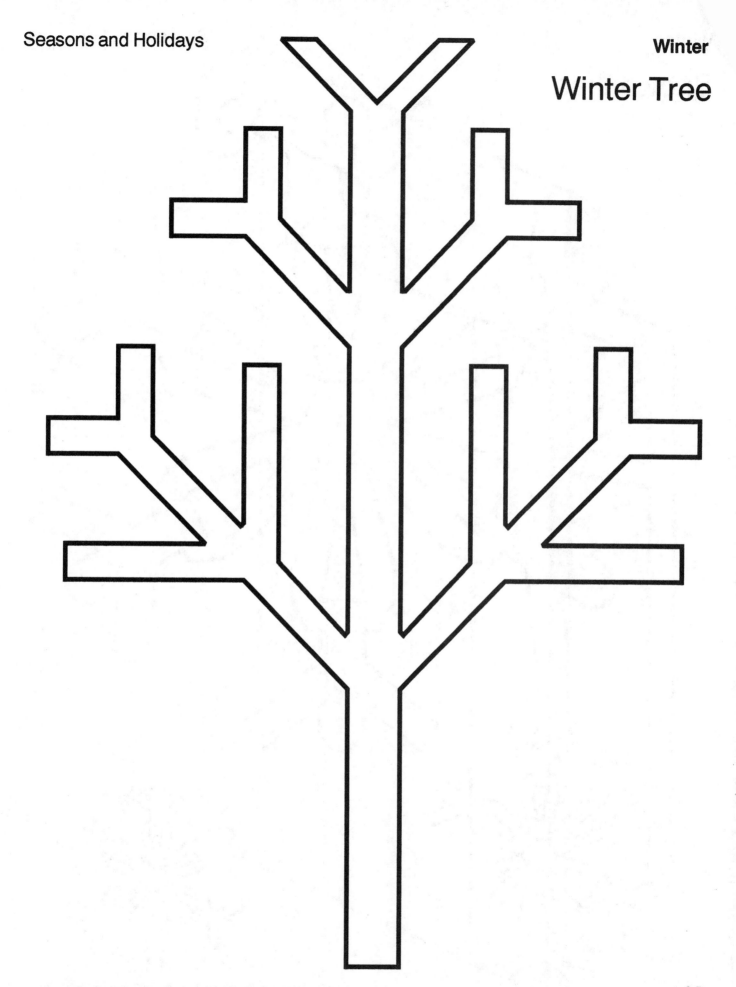

Snowflakes

Ice Skate

Mitten

The Giant Book of Theme Patterns © 1993 Fearon Teacher Aids

Groundhog

Daisy

Tulip

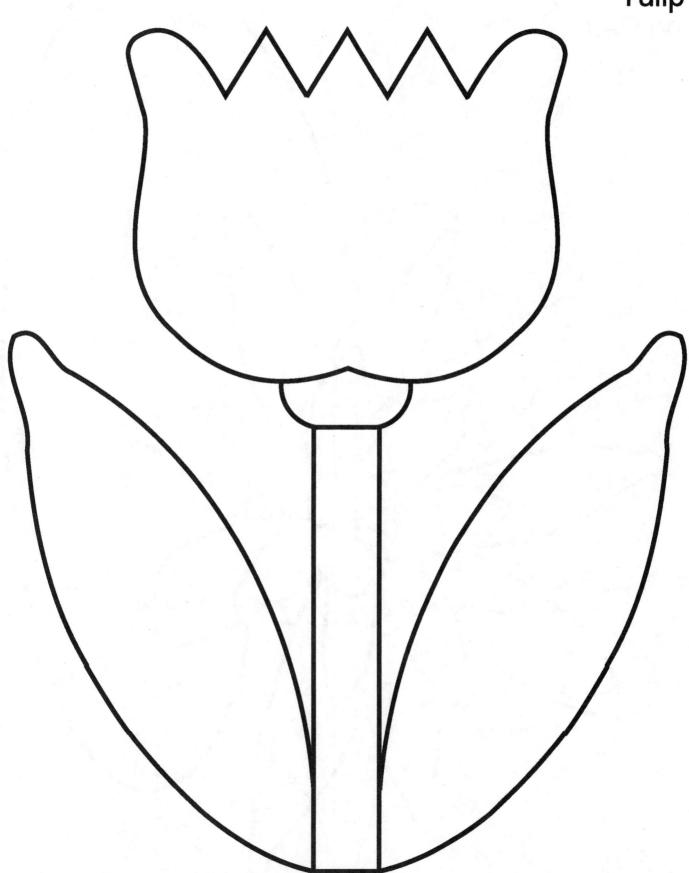

Water Lily
on Pad

Rose

Kite

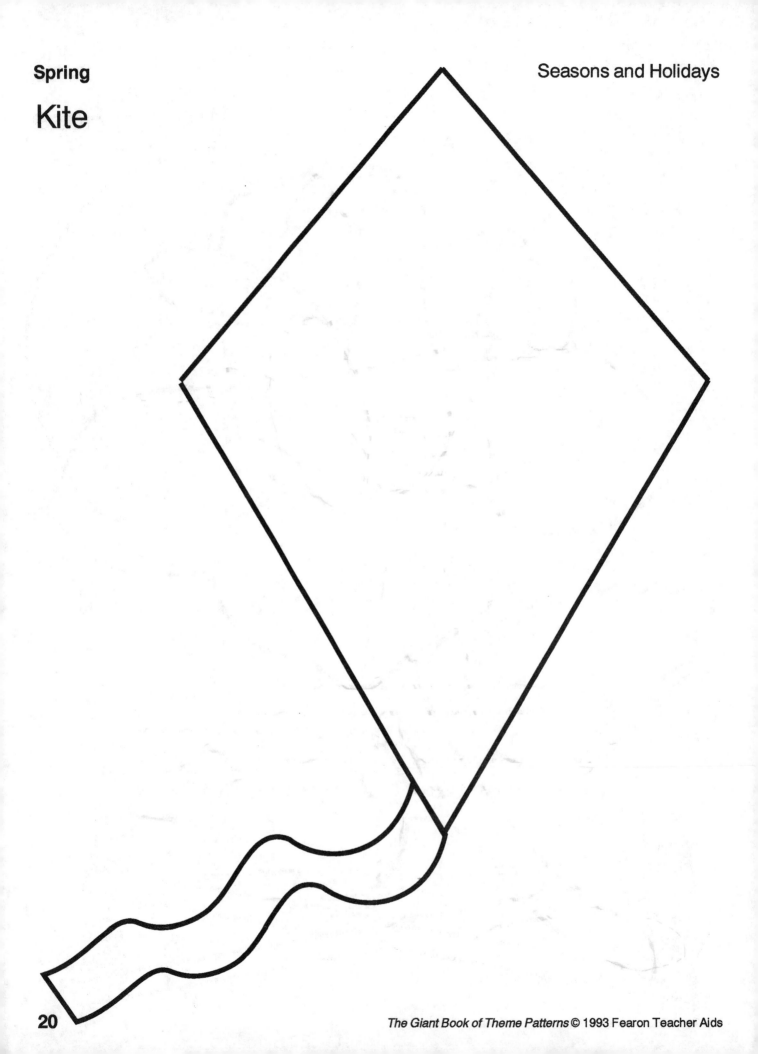

Weather Vane

Rainbow

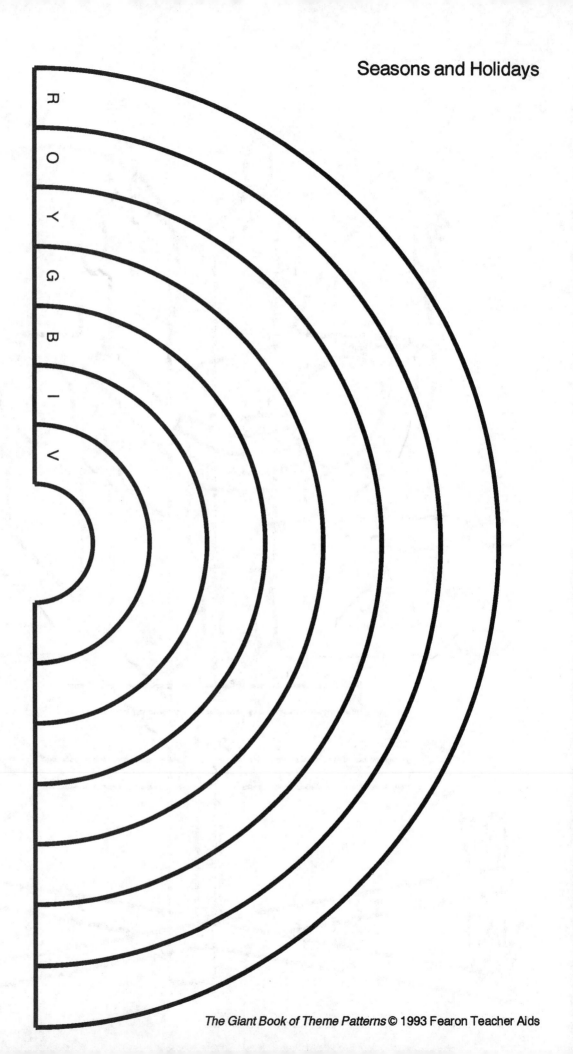

Spring Tree

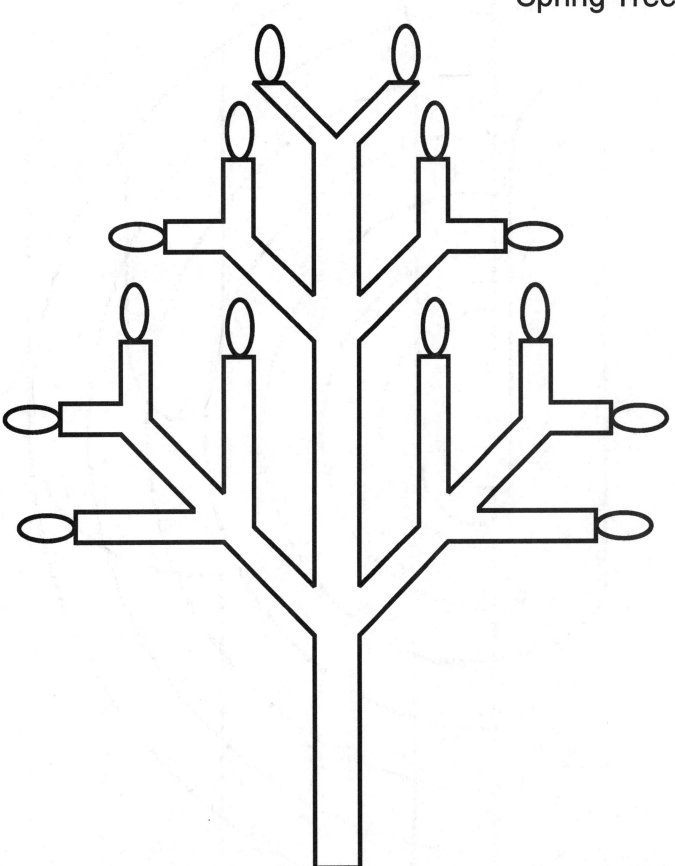

Cactus

Beach
Ball,
Bucket,
and
Shovel

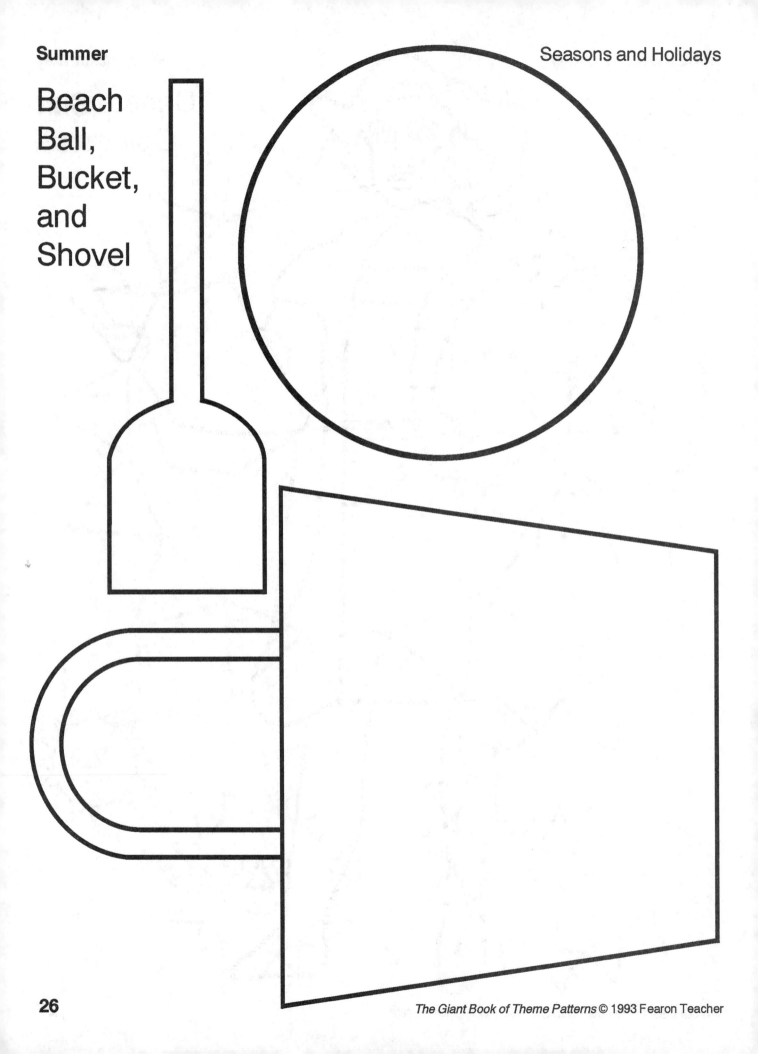

Christopher Columbus

Christopher Columbus Portrait

The Giant Book of Theme Patterns © 1993 Fearon Teacher

Niña, Pinta, and Santa Maria

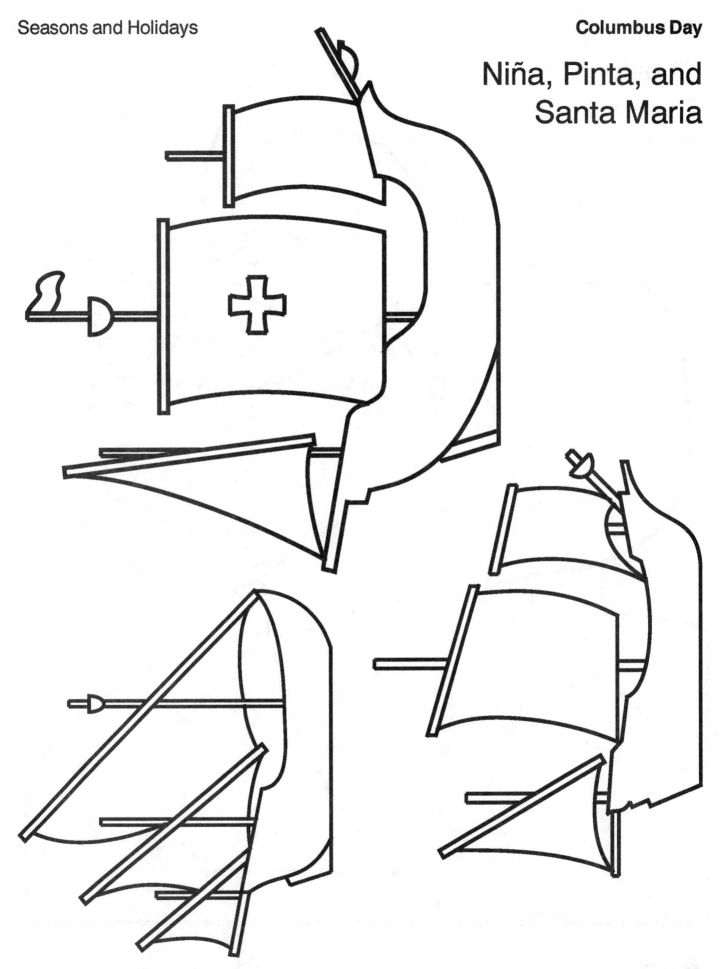

Ghost

Witch on a Broom

Witch (Head)

The Giant Book of Theme Patterns © 1993 Fearon Teacher

Jack–o'–Lantern

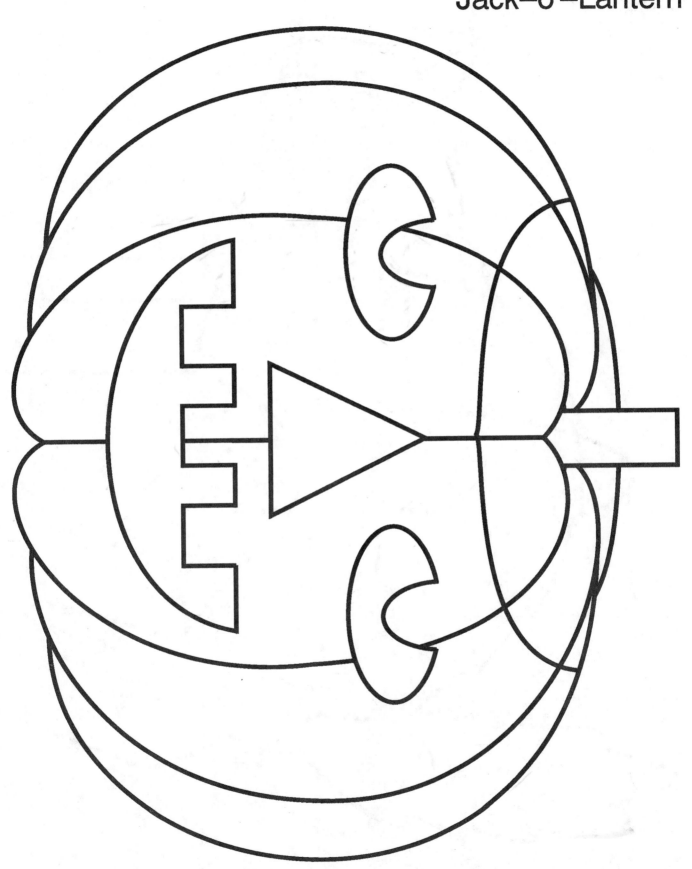

Black Cat

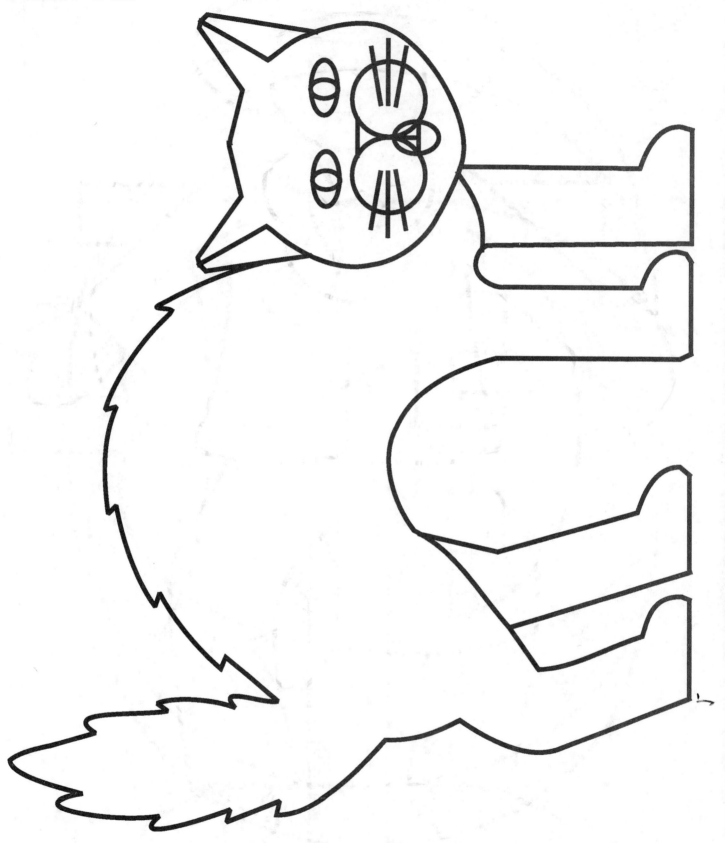

Scarecrow

Skeleton

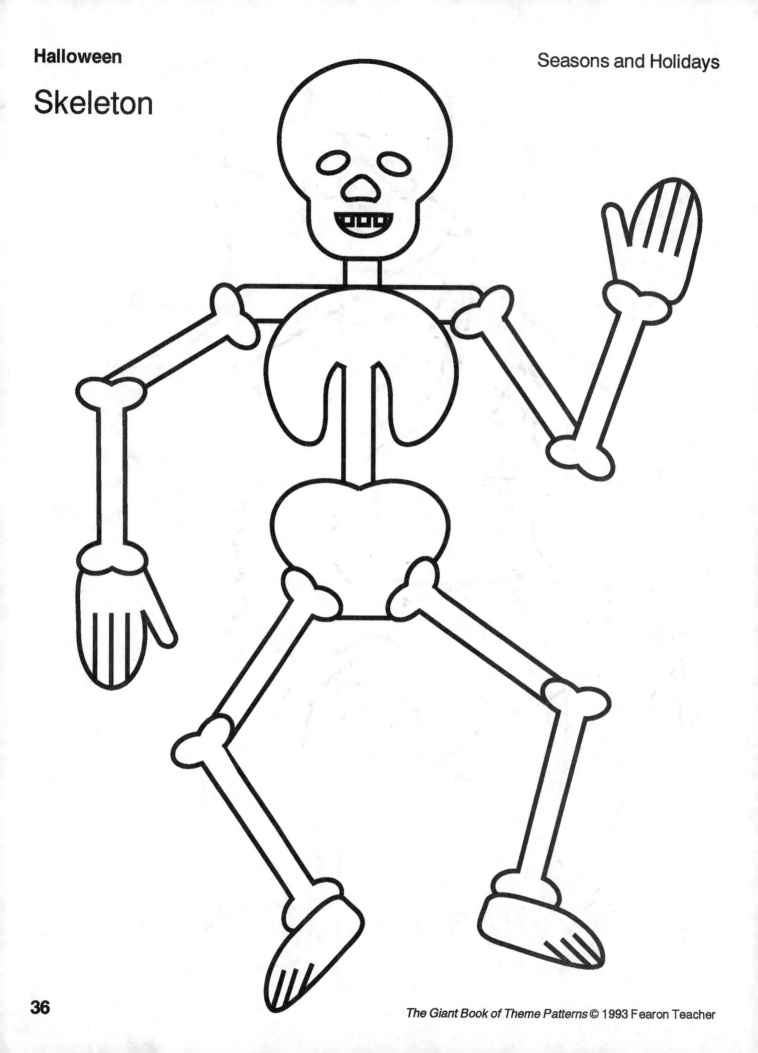

Bat

Owl

Sailor

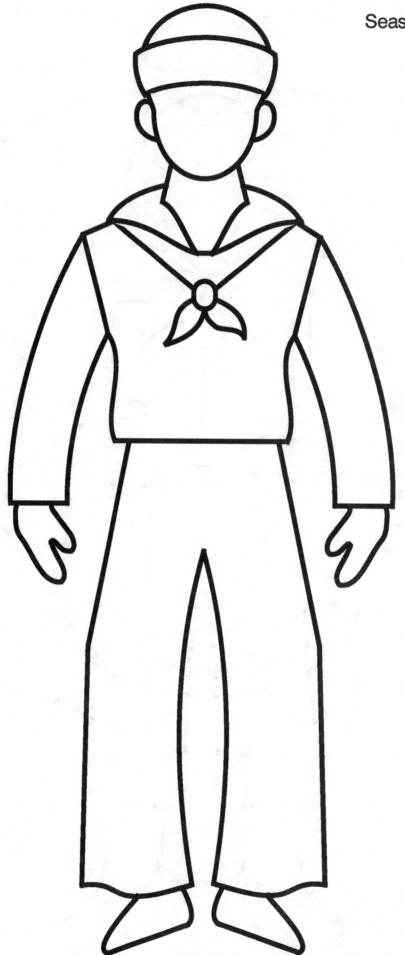

Soldier

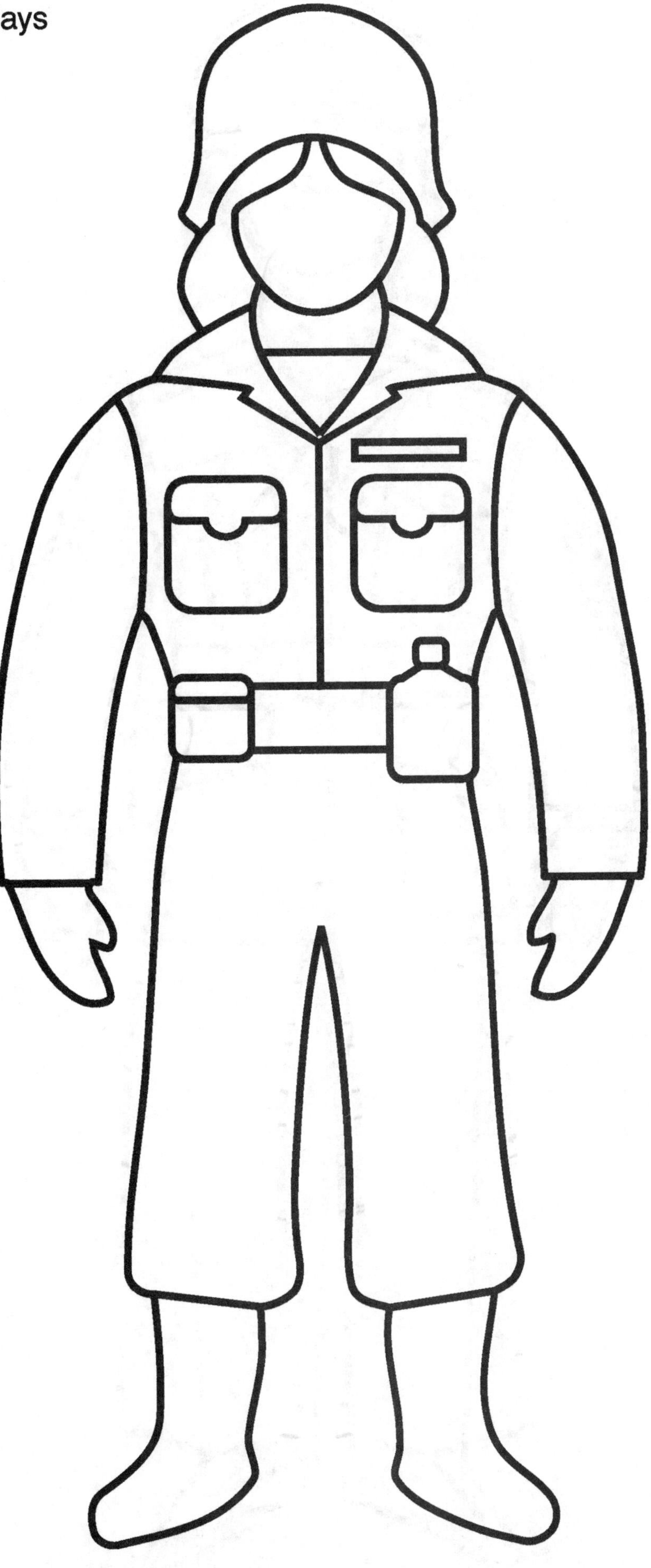

Marine

The Giant Book of Theme Patterns © 1993 Fearon Teacher

Pilgrim Man

Pilgrim Woman

Mayflower

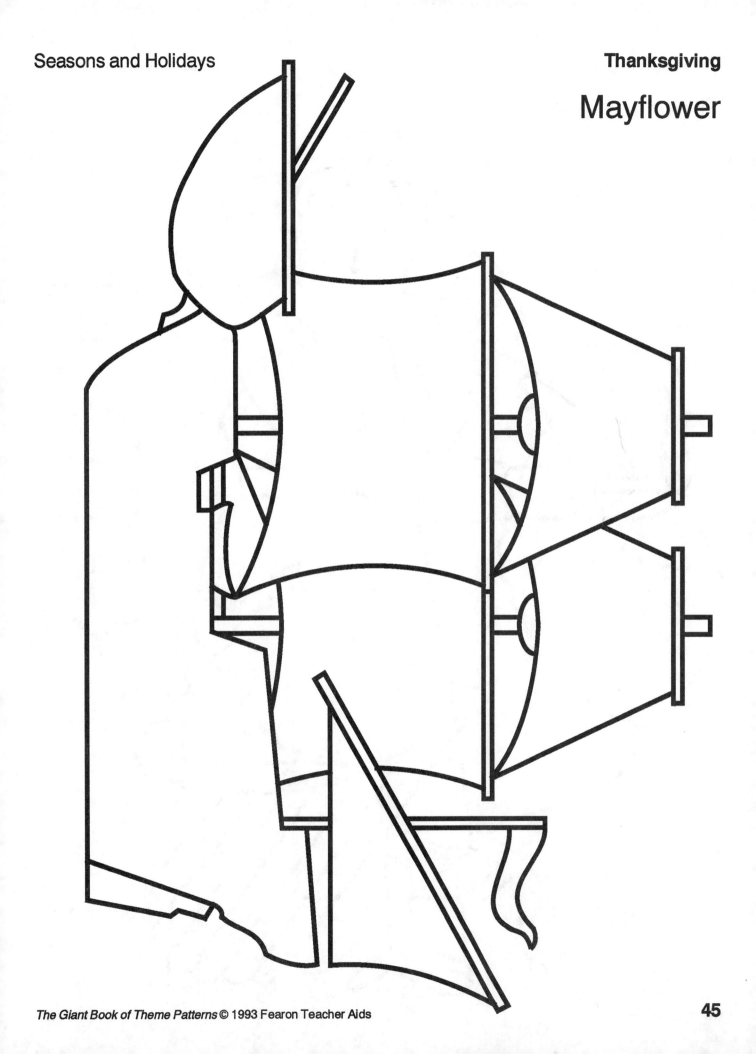

Turkey

Indian Brave
and Maiden

Indian in a Canoe

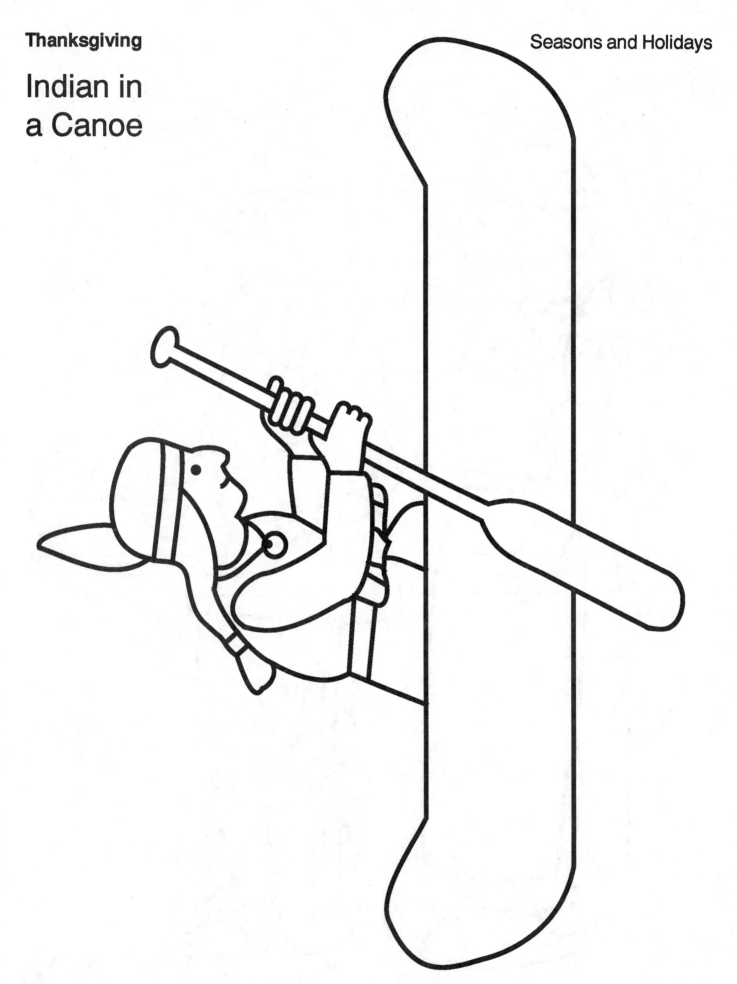

Mistletoe

Holly

Stars

Bells

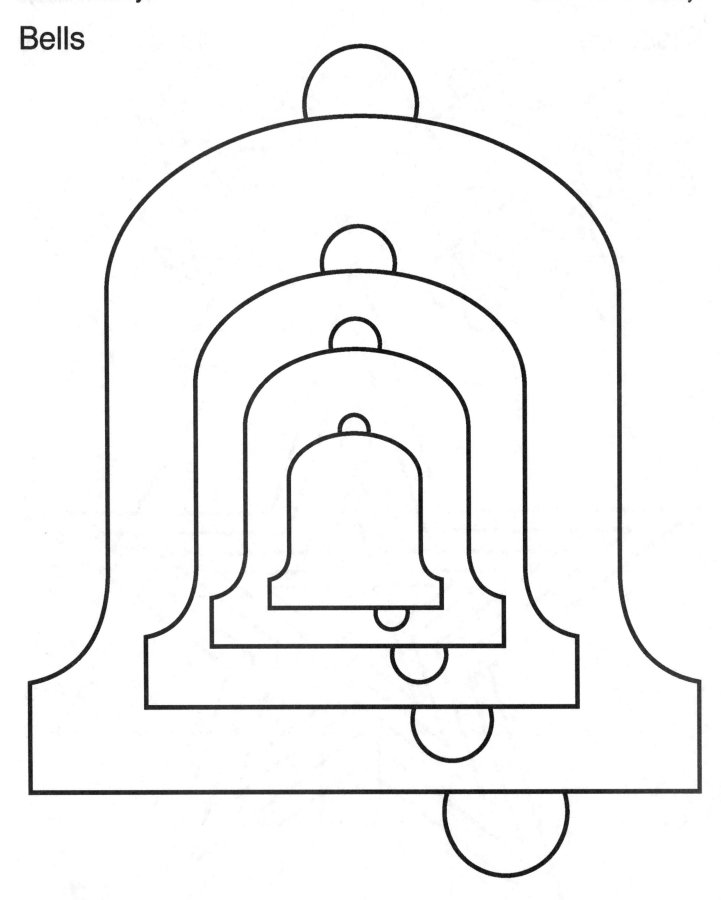

Christmas Tree

Wreath

Stockings

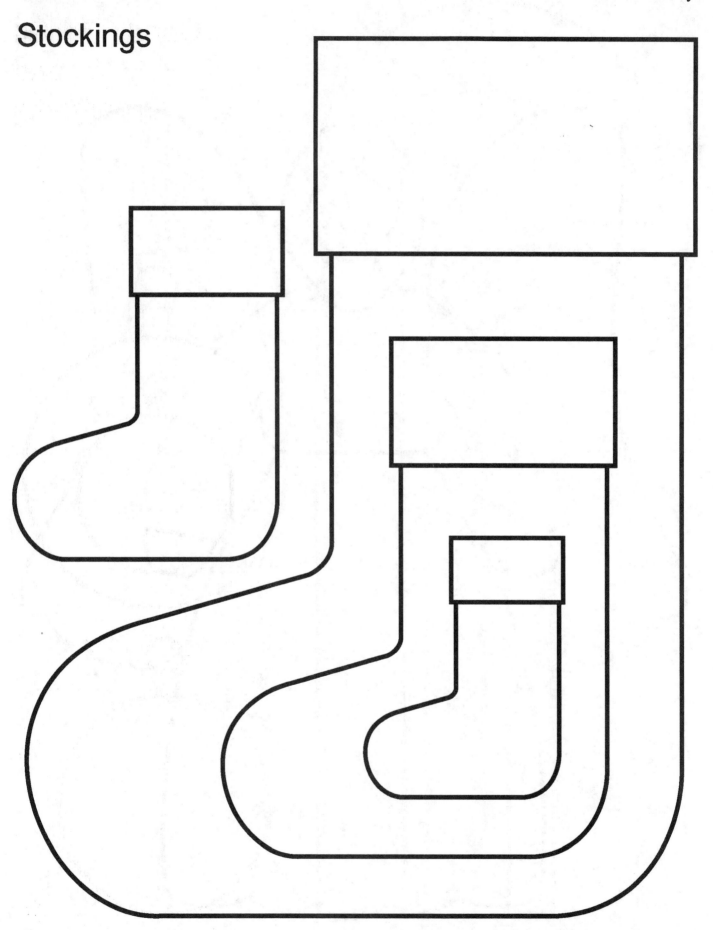

Candy Canes
and
Ornaments

Present

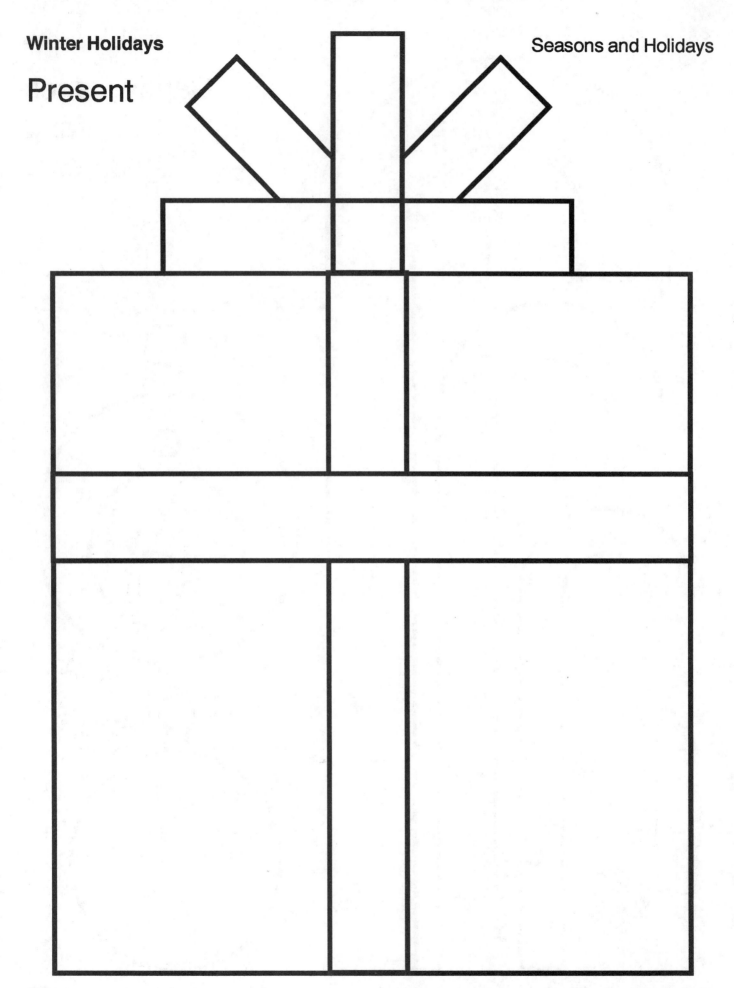

The Giant Book of Theme Patterns © 1993 Fearon Teacher Aids

Santa Claus

Reindeer
and Sleigh

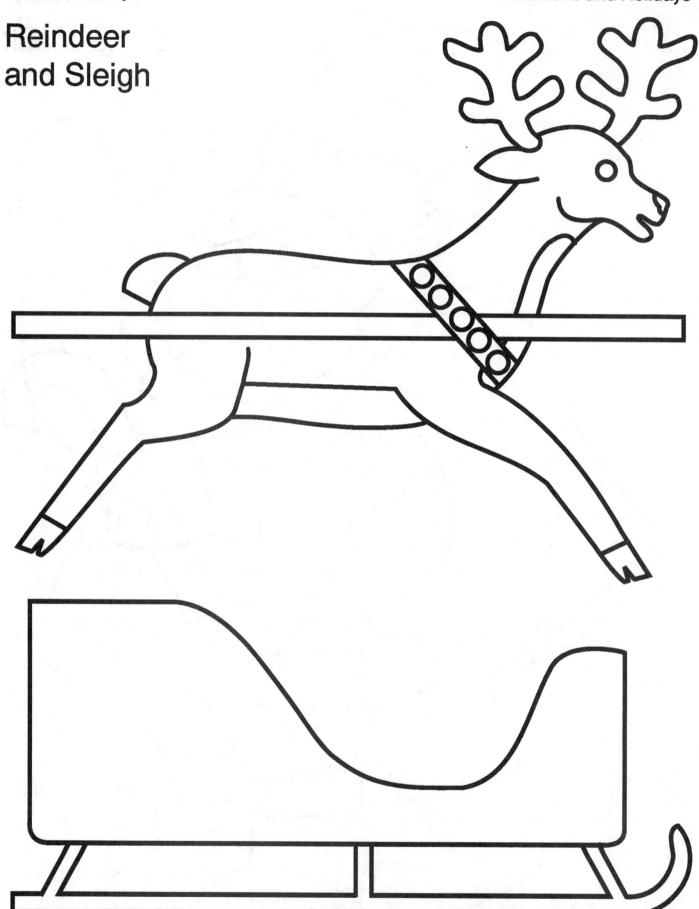

Elf

Menorah
and Dreidel

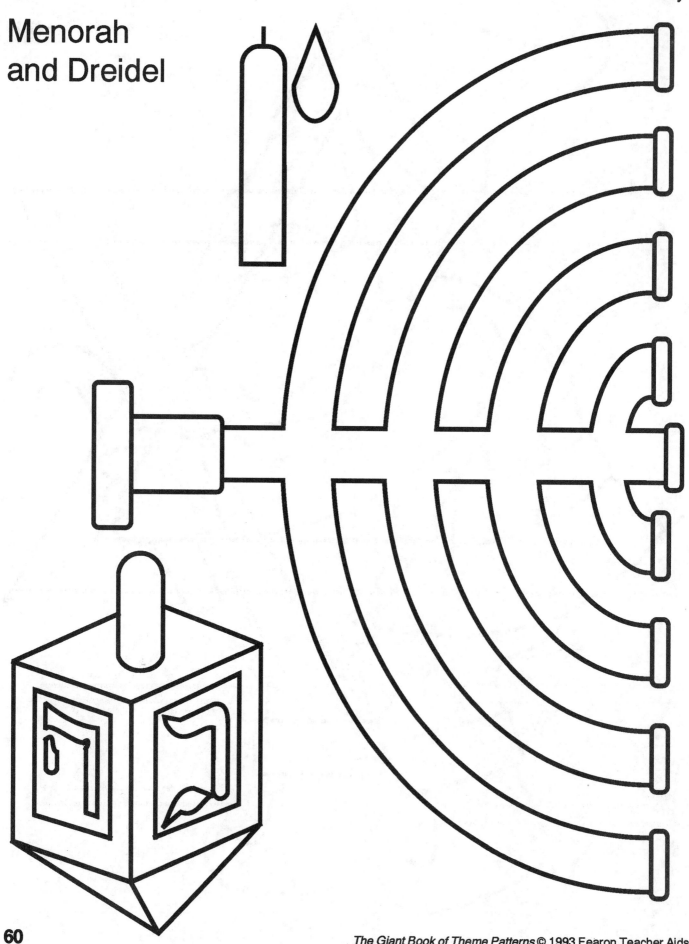

Star of David

Piñata

Father Time

Clock

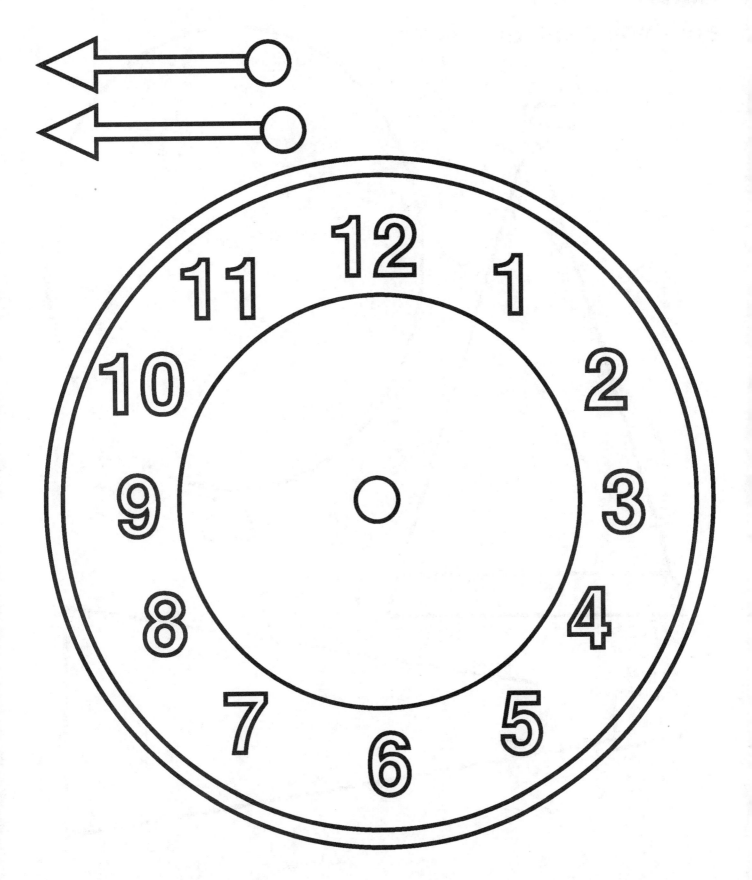

Hat, Balloon, and Noisemaker

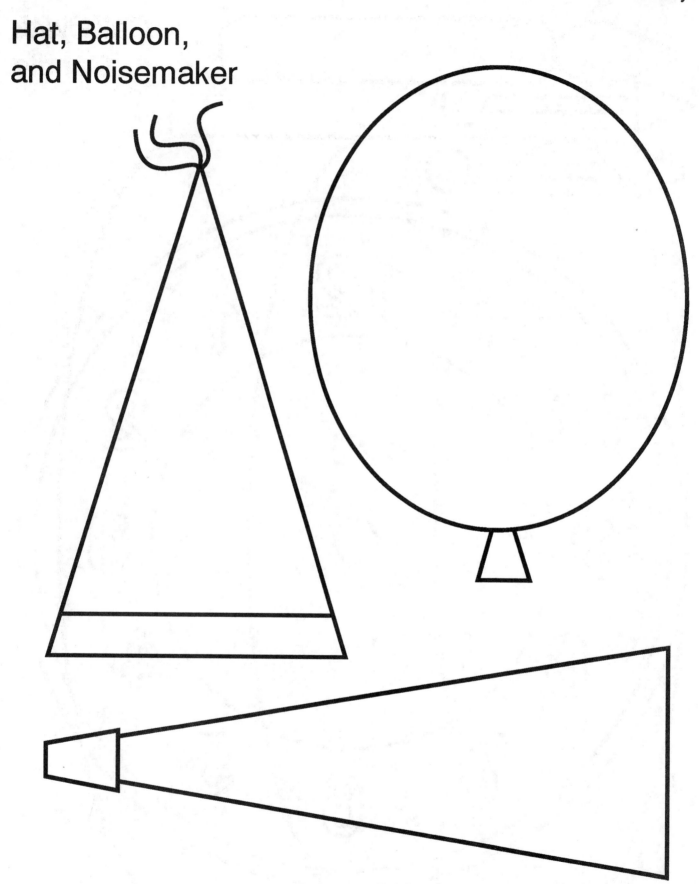

Cake with Candle

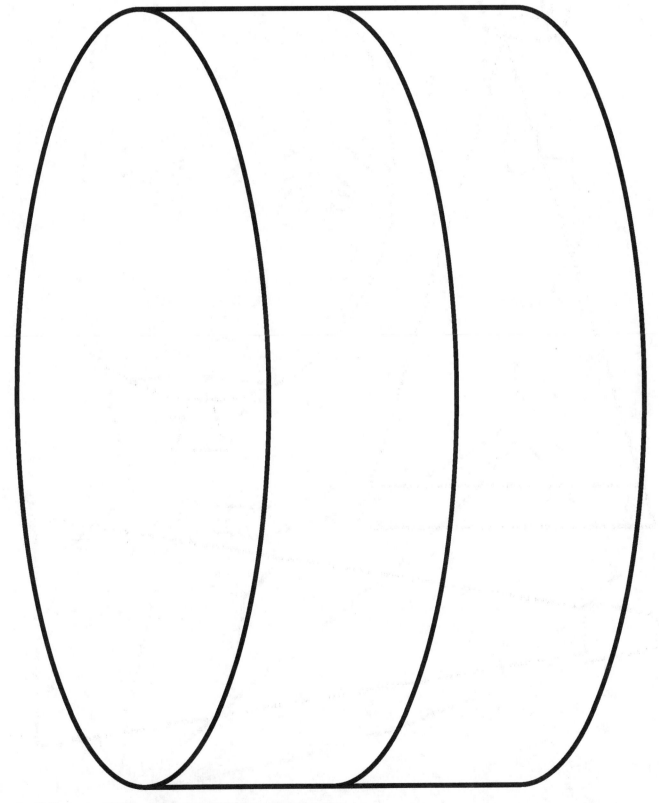

Martin
Luther
King, Jr.

Children
Holding
Hands

"I Have a Dream. . . ."

Abraham
Lincoln

Abraham Lincoln in Profile

Log Cabin

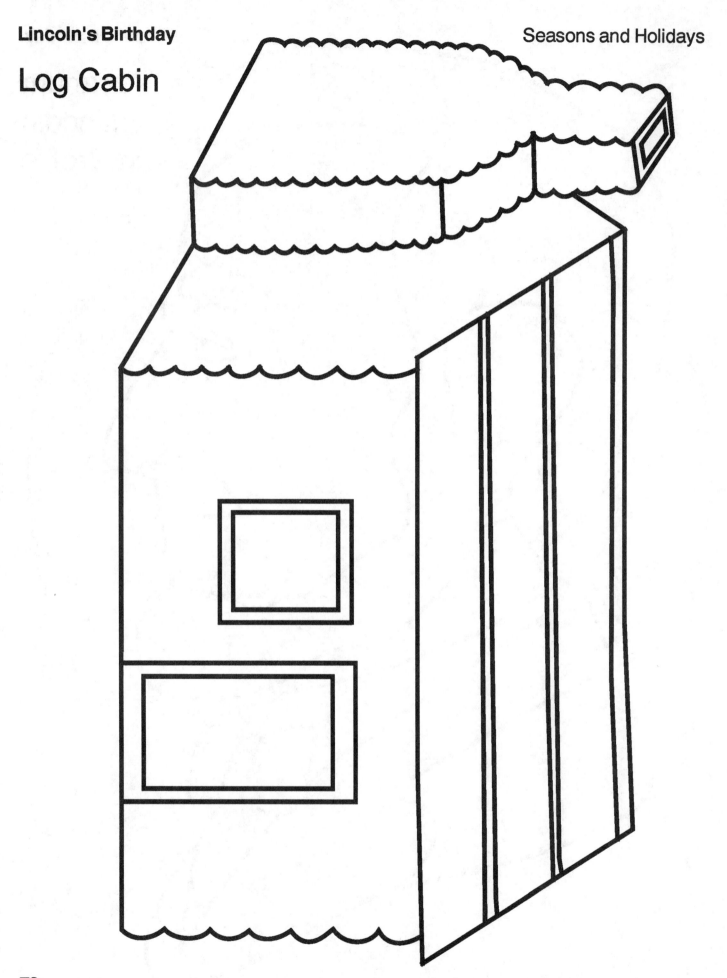

The Giant Book of Theme Patterns © 1993 Fearon Teacher Aids

Be My Valentine

*Be My
Valentine*

Cupid

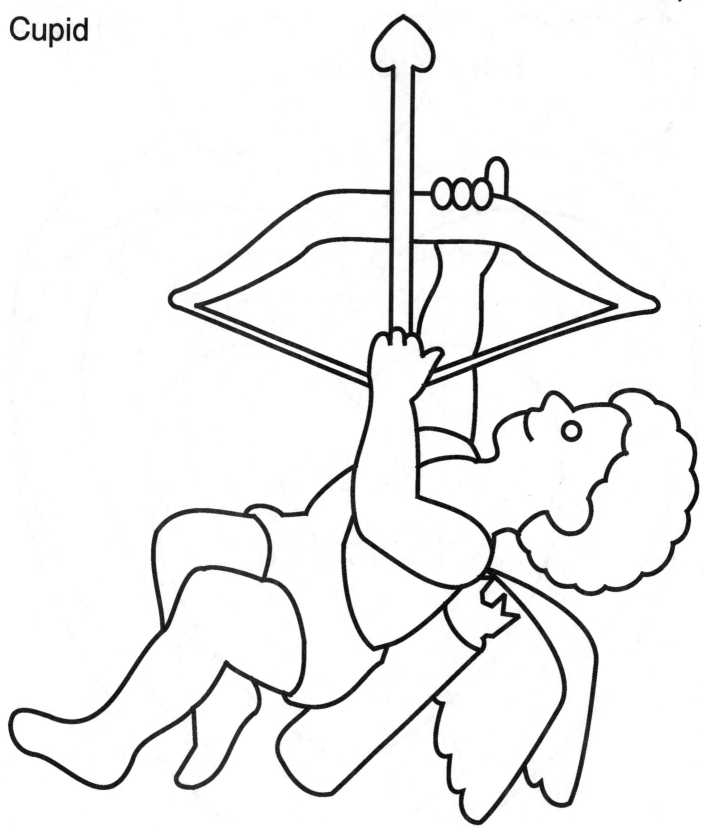

Hearts

George Washington

George Washington in Profile

Hatchet and Cherry Tree

The Giant Book of Theme Patterns © 1993 Fearon Teacher Aids

Shamrocks

Leprechaun

Easter Basket
and Candy

Easter Bunny

The Giant Book of Theme Patterns © 1993 Fearon Teacher Aids

Easter Eggs

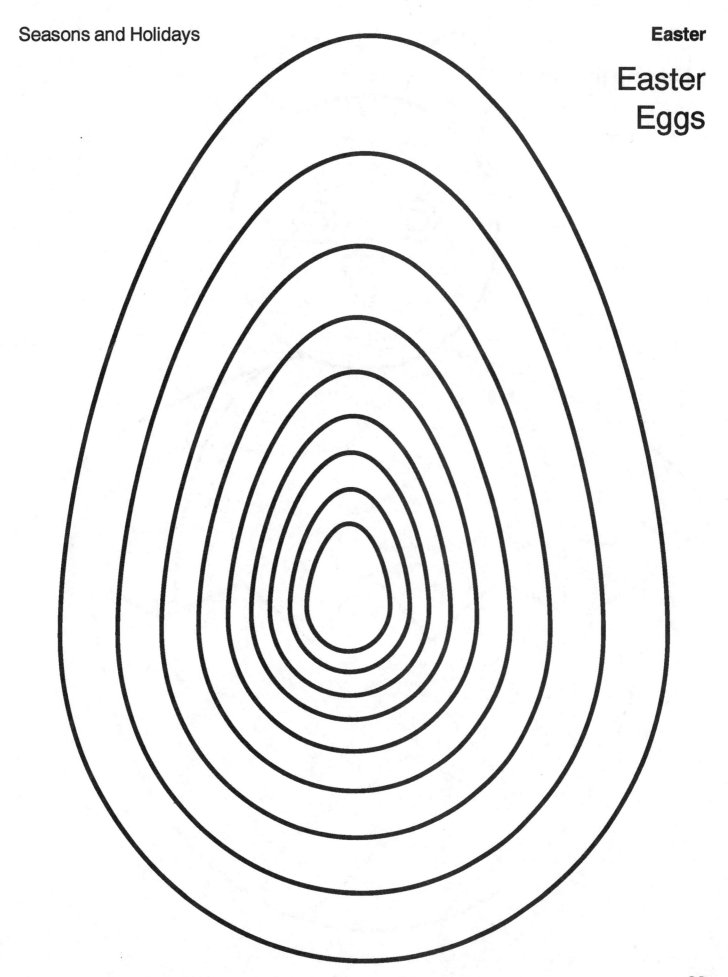

Hatching Chick

The Giant Book of Theme Patterns © 1993 Fearon Teacher Aids

Mother with Corsage

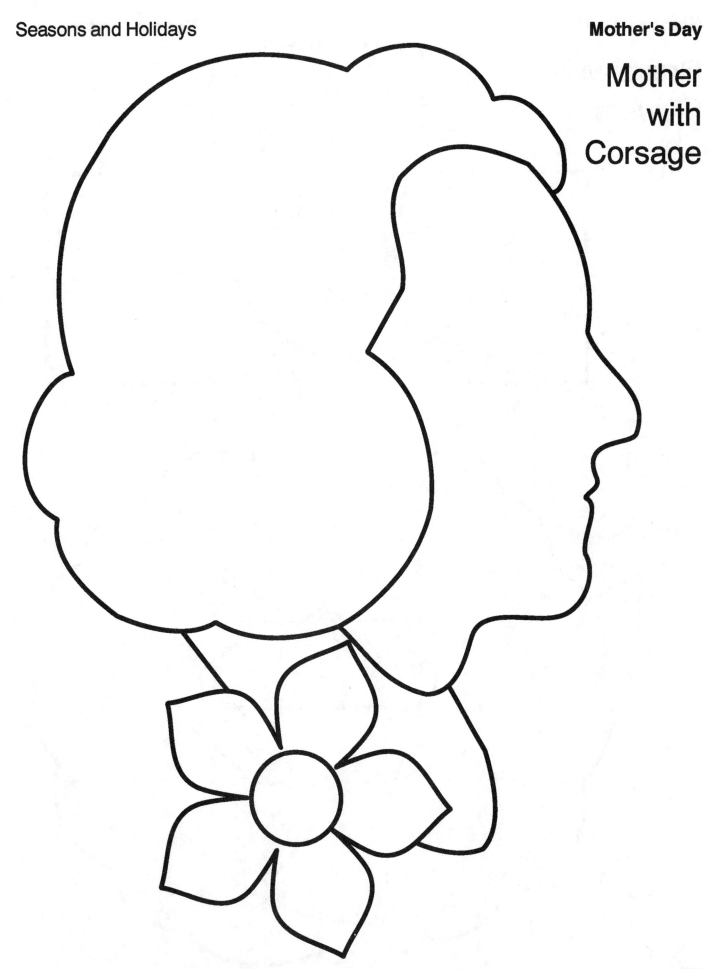

Grave with Flowers

American Flag

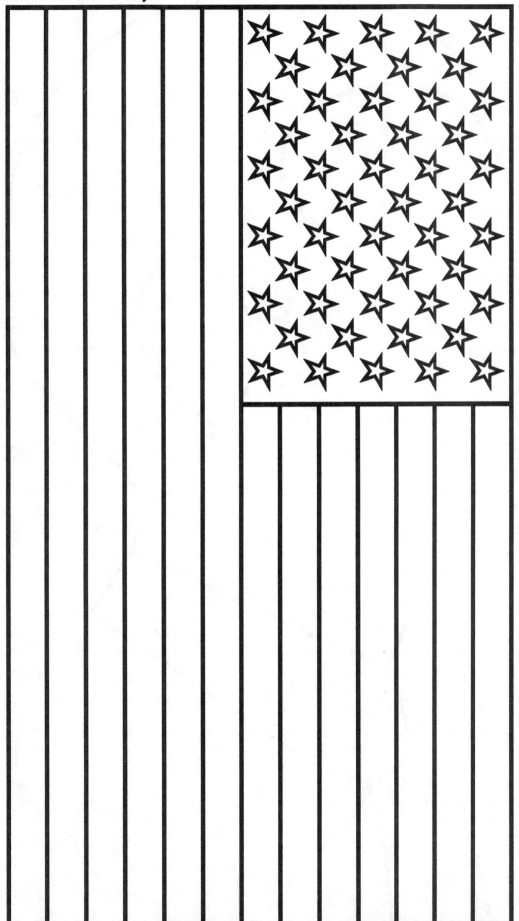

Father with New Tie

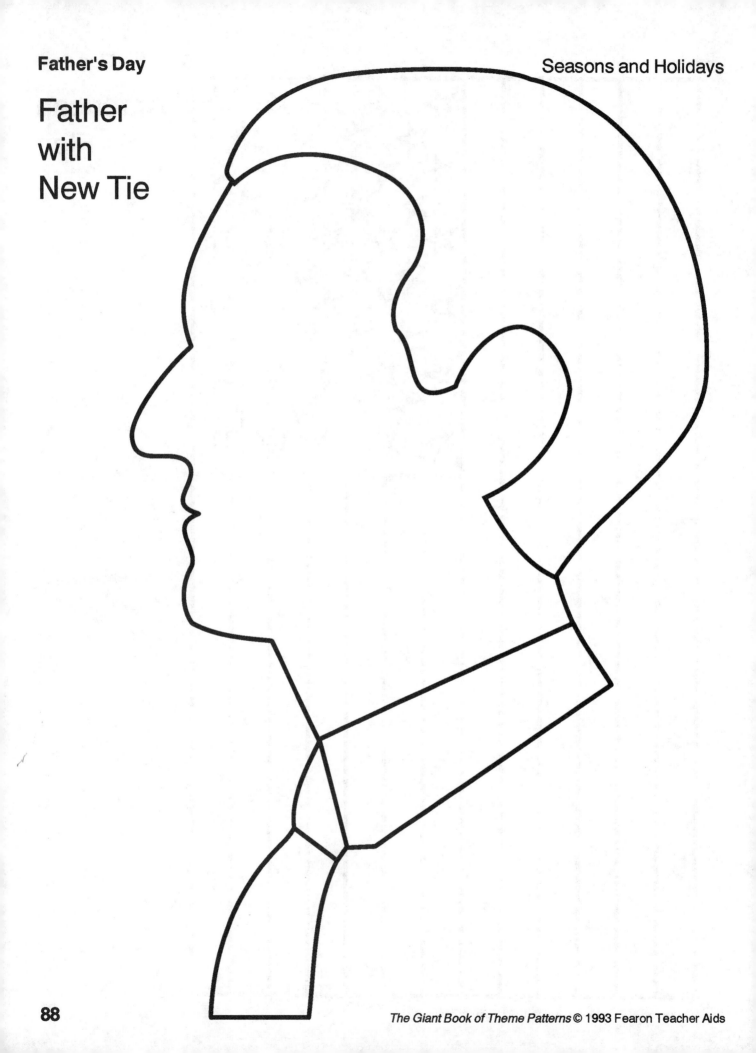

Firecracker

BANG!

Uncle Sam

Anteater

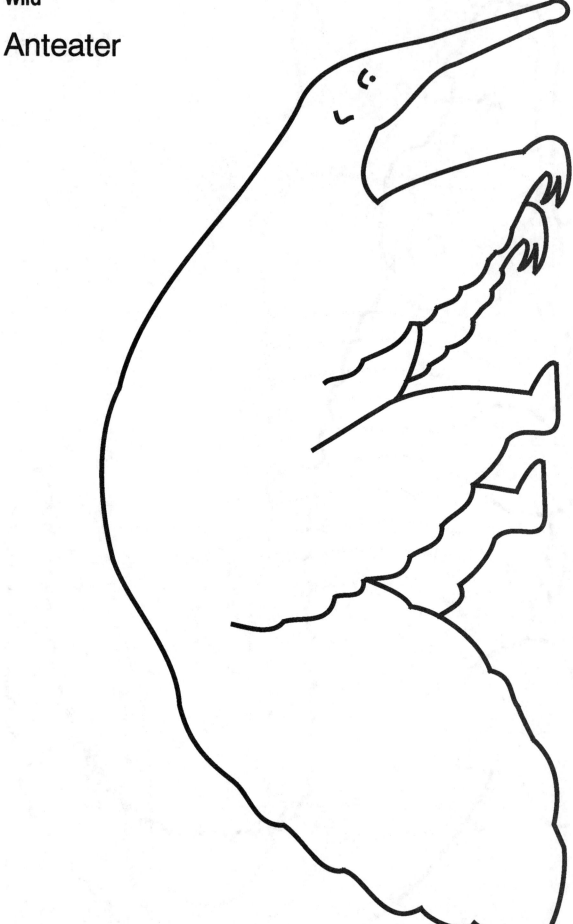

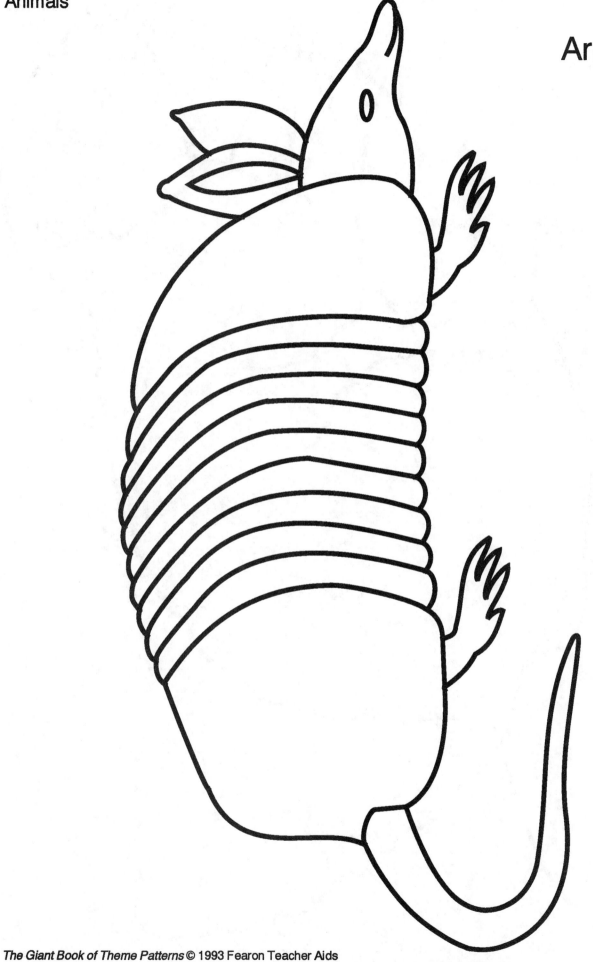

Beaver

Buffalo

California Condor

Make a flopped duplicate
of wing and attach here.

Finished California condor
will look like this. Remove
excess lines within body.

Chipmunk

Crocodile

Deer

Frog

Frog
Life Cycle

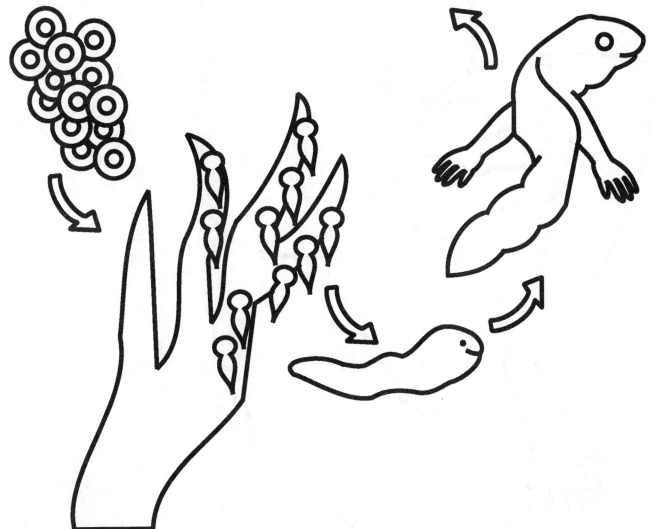

Fox

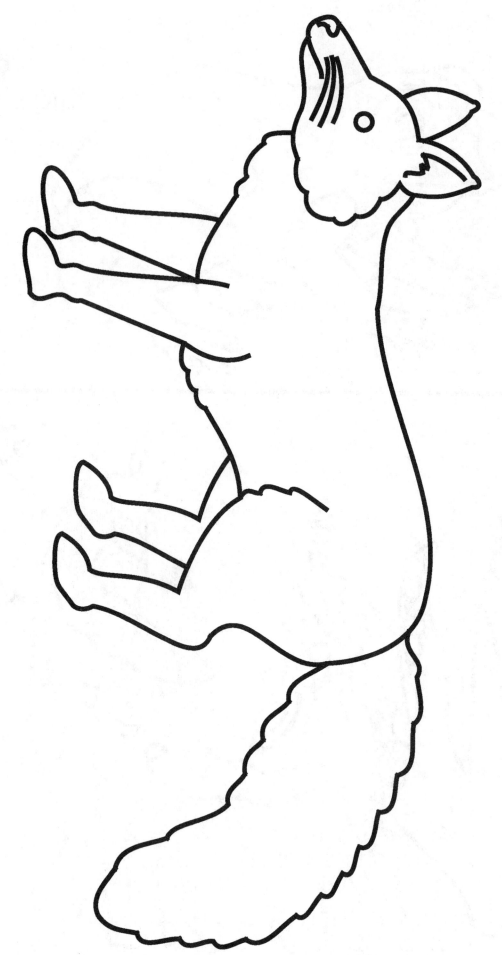

Gorilla

Hippopotamus

Kangaroo

Finished kangaroo will
look like the above.

Attach tail here.

Koala

Lion

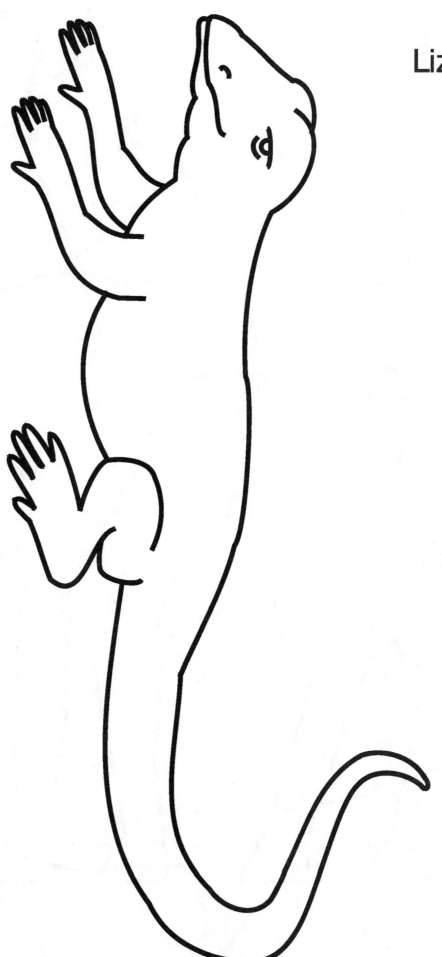

Llama

Moose

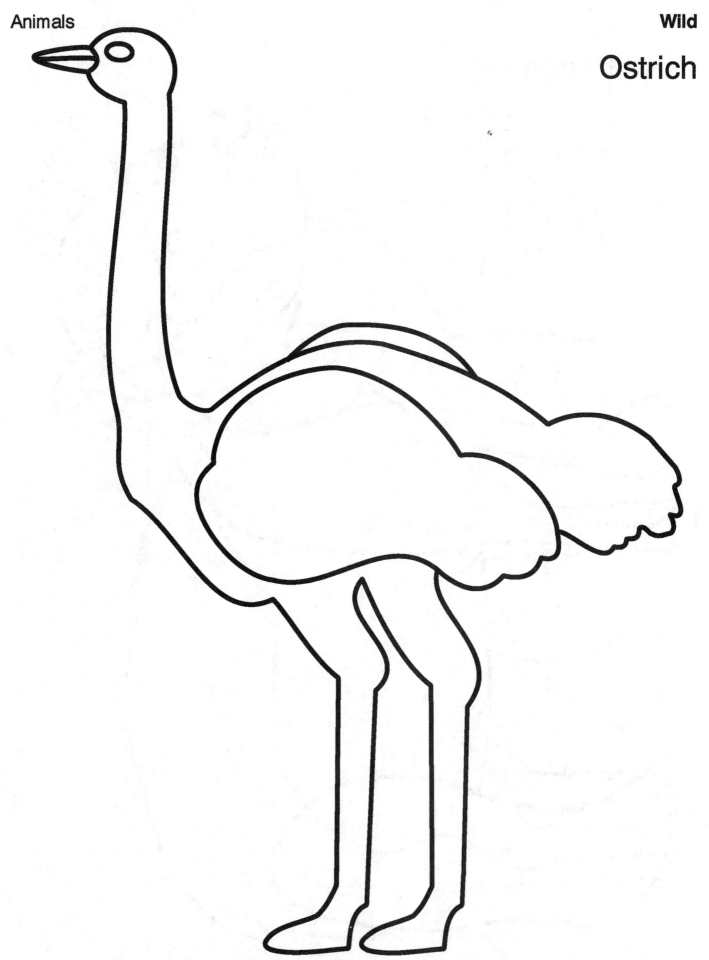

Giant Panda

Finished peacock will look like the above.

Make duplicate of tail. Place two pieces
together to make completed tail. Place
body on tail for completed peacock.

Polar Bear

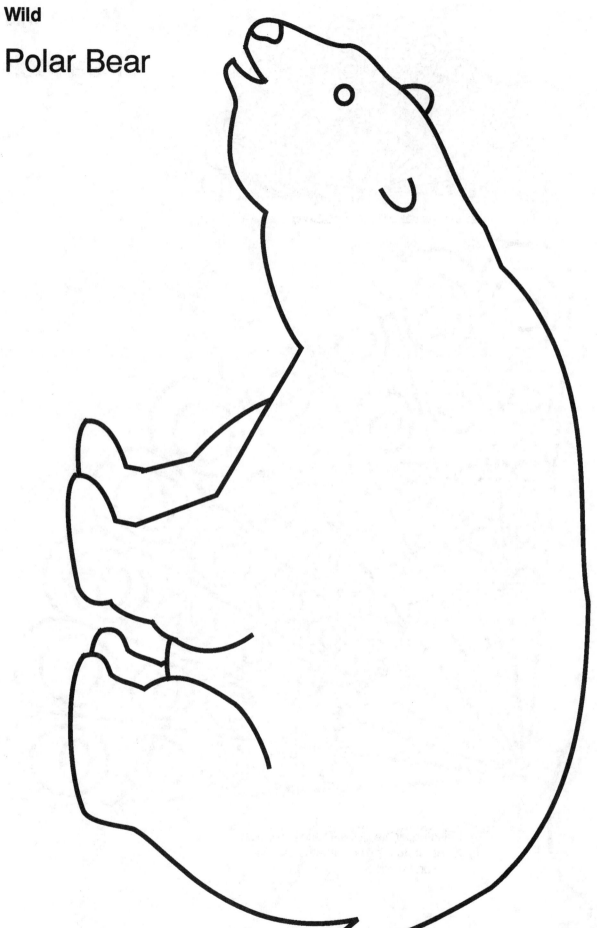

Porcupine

Quail

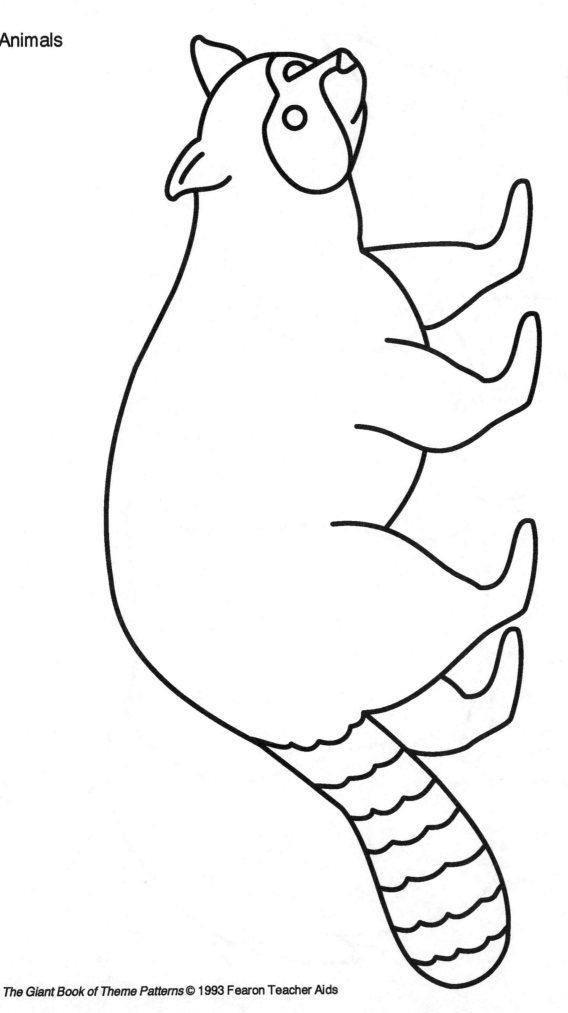

Rhinoceros

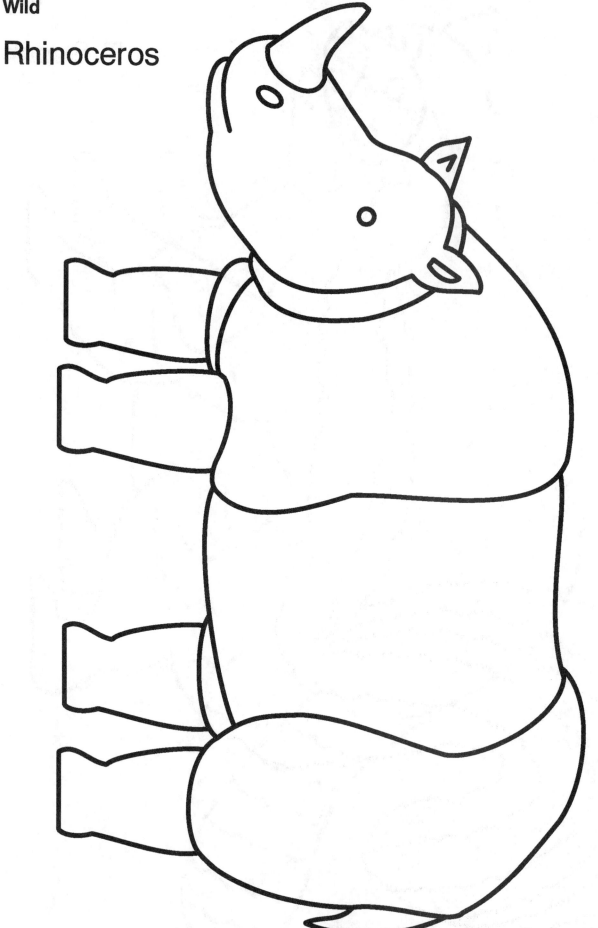

Skunk

Squirrel

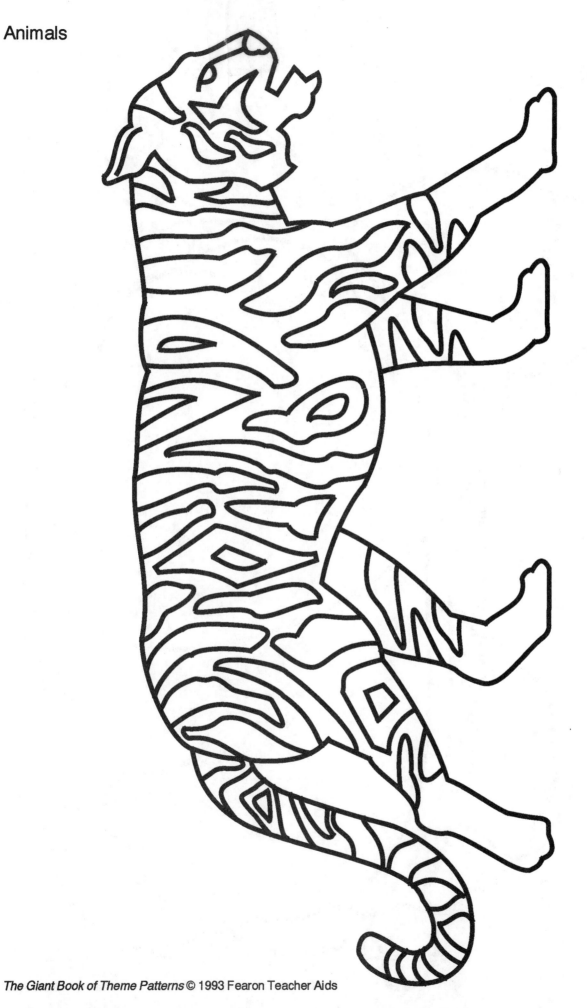

Tortoise

Zebra

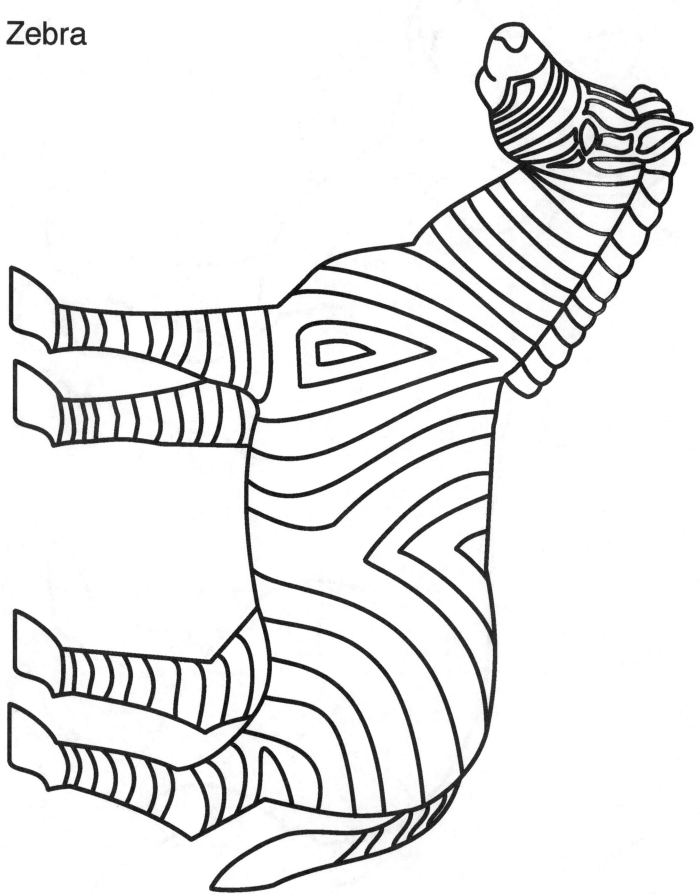

Cat

Cockatoo

Collie

Fish

Fishbowl

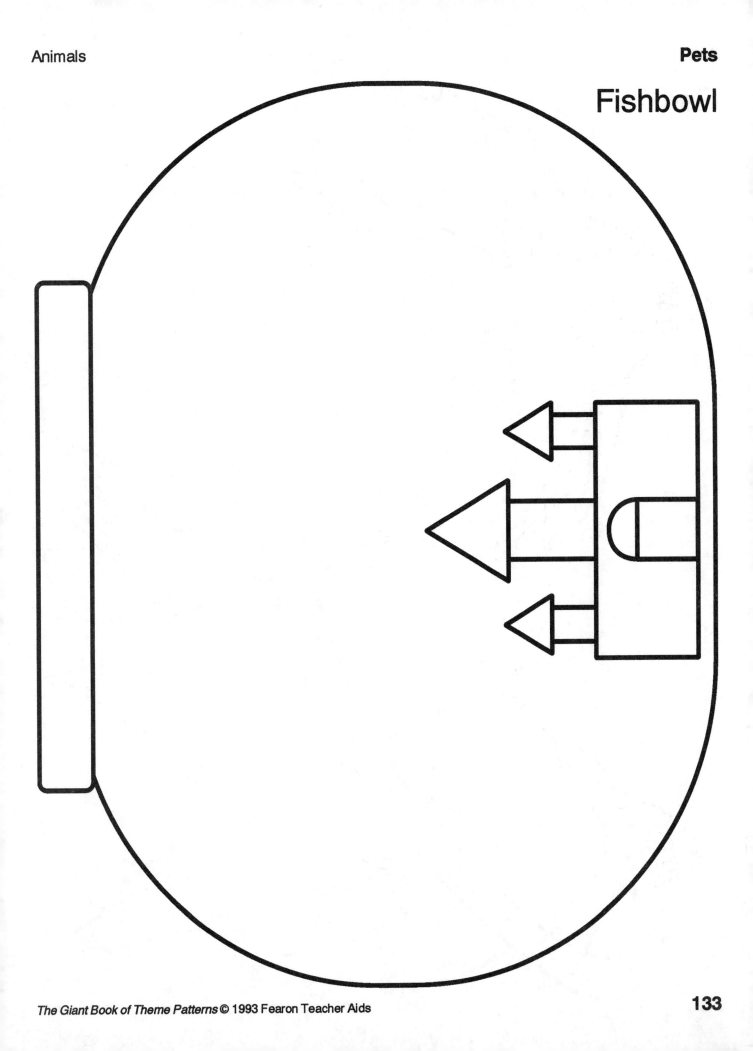

Gerbil

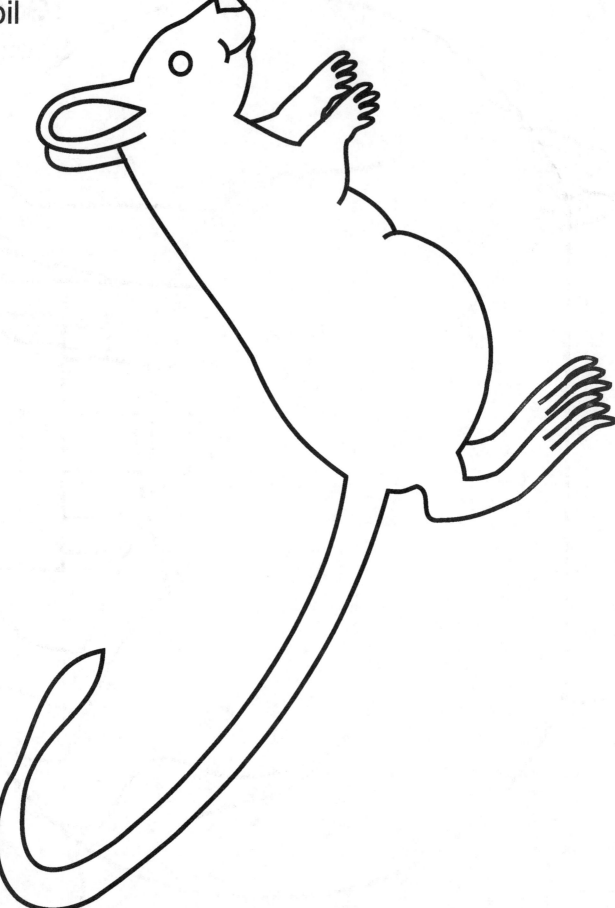

German
Shepherd

Kitten

Poodle

Puppy

Scottie
and Beagle

The Giant Book of Theme Patterns © 1993 Fearon Teacher Aids

Blue Whale

Water Spout

Dolphin

Lobster

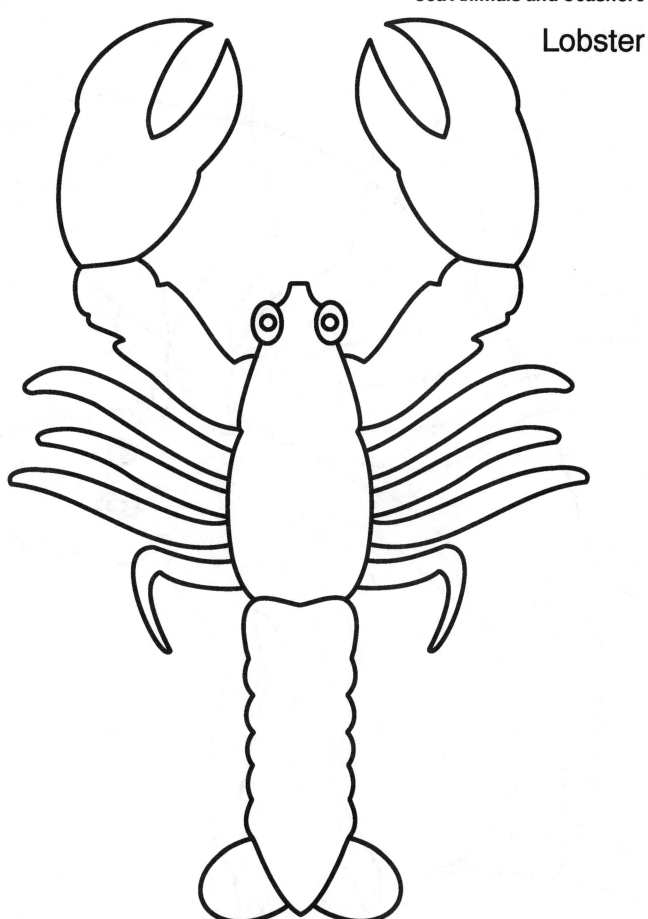

Octopus

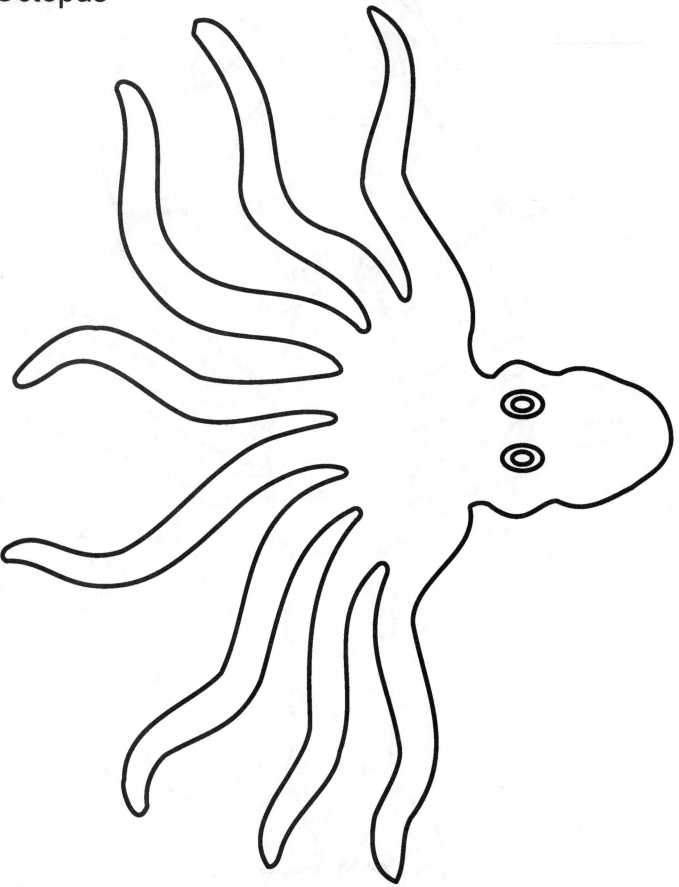

Penguin

Sea Horse

Seal

Sea Lion

Sea Otter

Sea Turtle

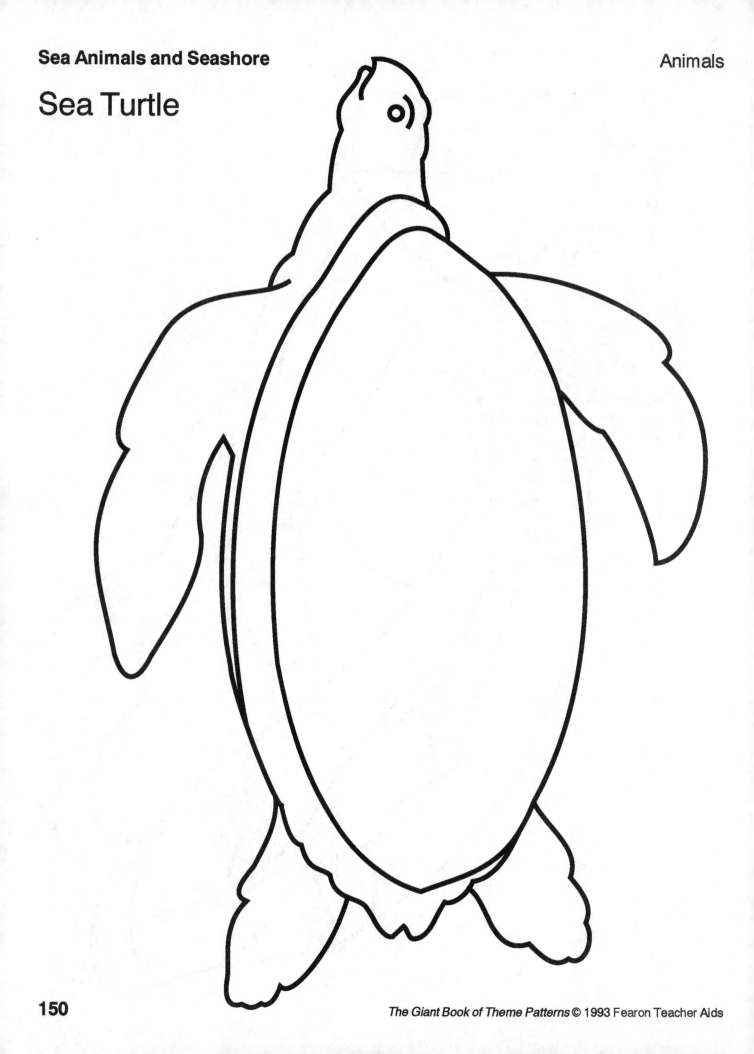

Shark

Saltwater Fish

Whale

Pelican

Sea Birds

Sea Gull

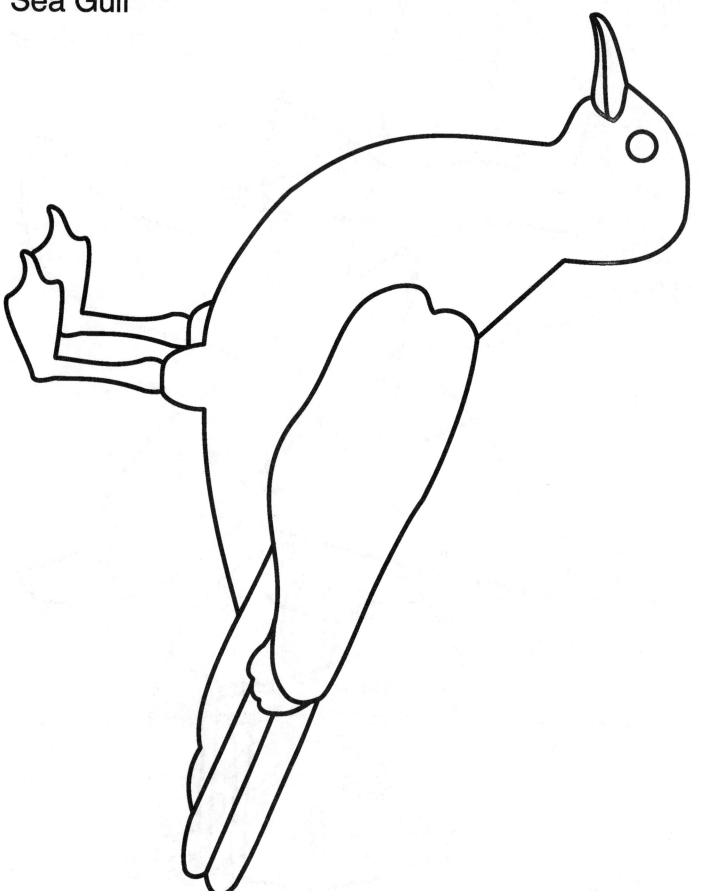

Starfish and Sand Dollar

Conch

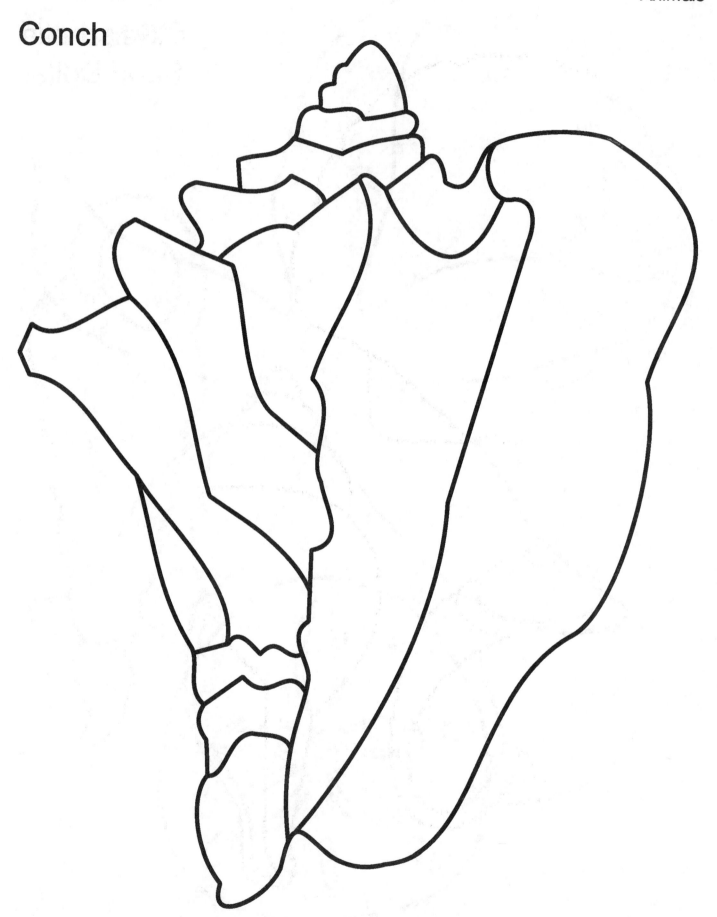

Seashells

Rabbit and Bunny

Cow
and Calf

Bull

Mare and Foal

Ewe and
Lamb

The Giant Book of Theme Patterns © 1993 Fearon Teacher Aids

Sow and Piglet

Hen and Chicks

Rooster

Duck and Ducklings

Swan

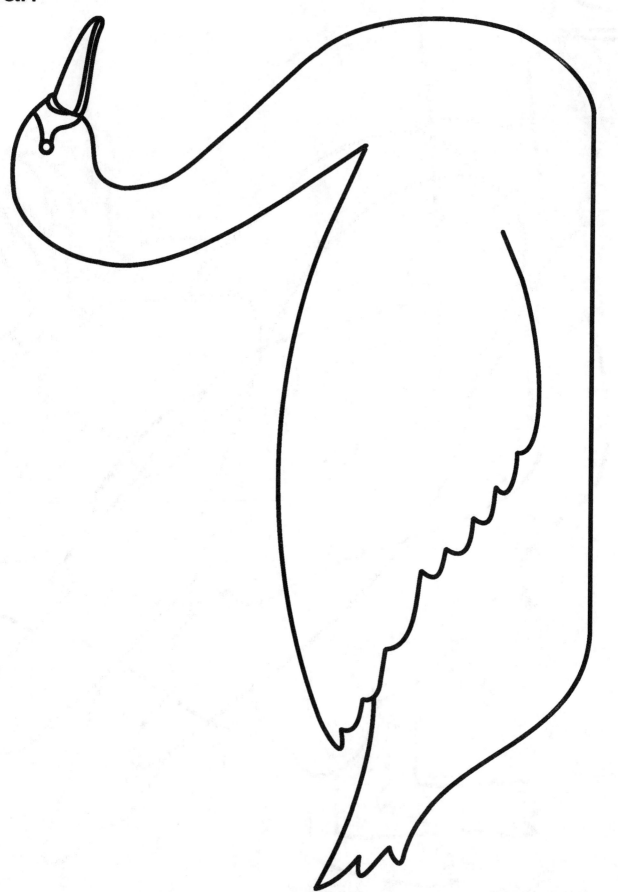

Bald Eagle

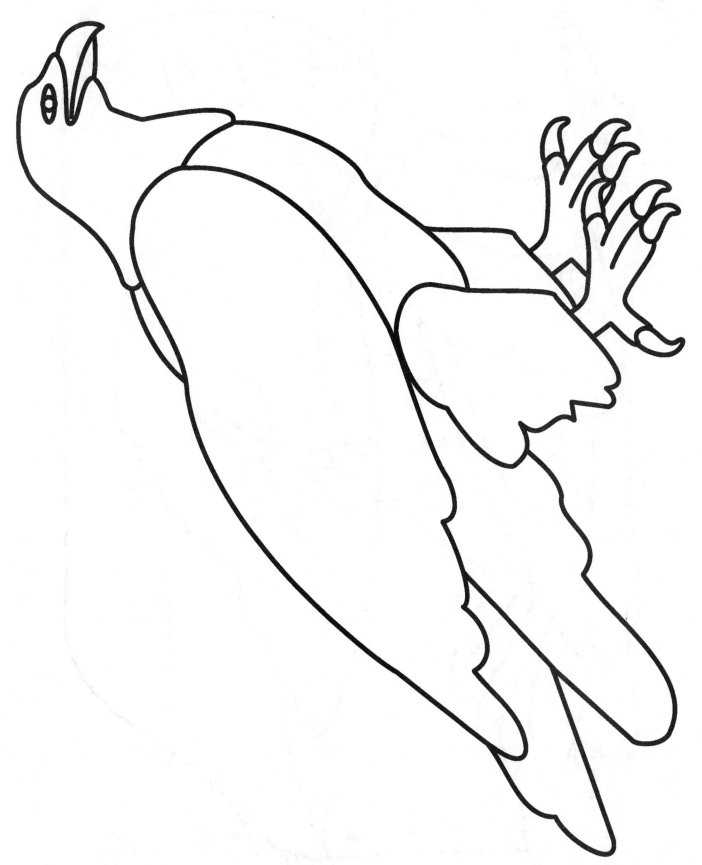

Woodpecker

Hummingbird and Feeder

Nest and Bird Egg

Nest with Mother
and Baby Birds

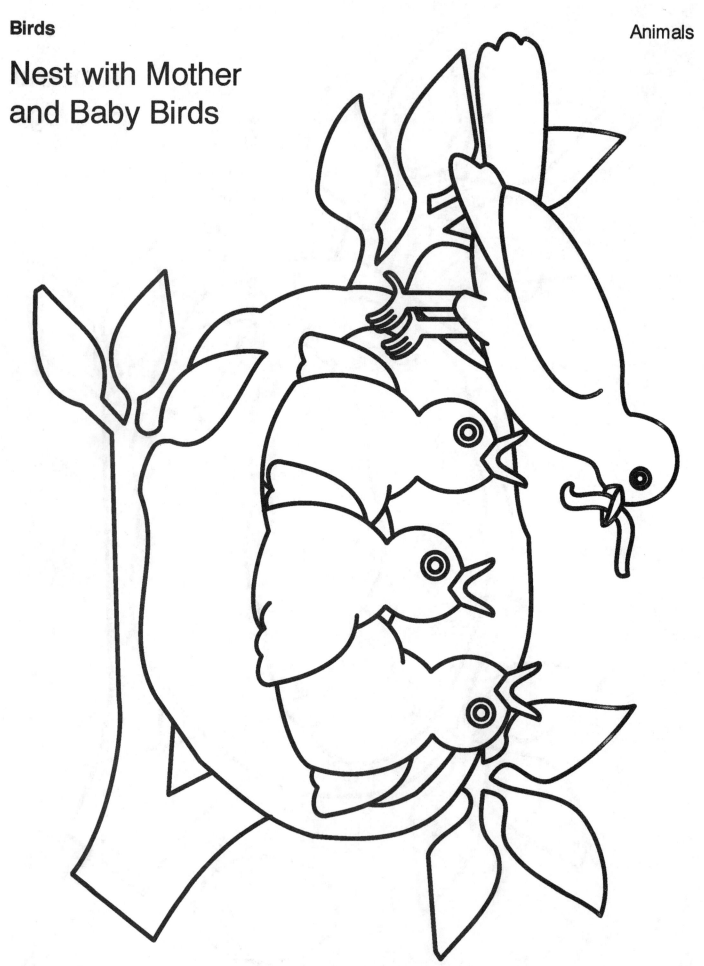

Grasshopper

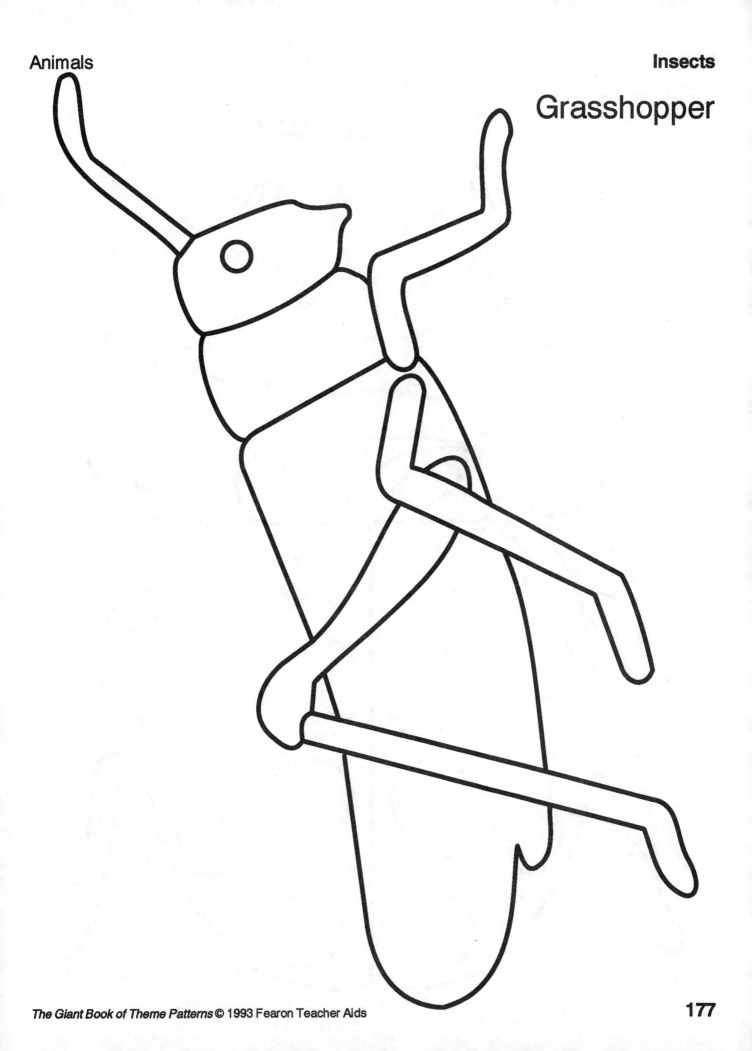

Ladybug

Hive and Honeybee

Butterfly

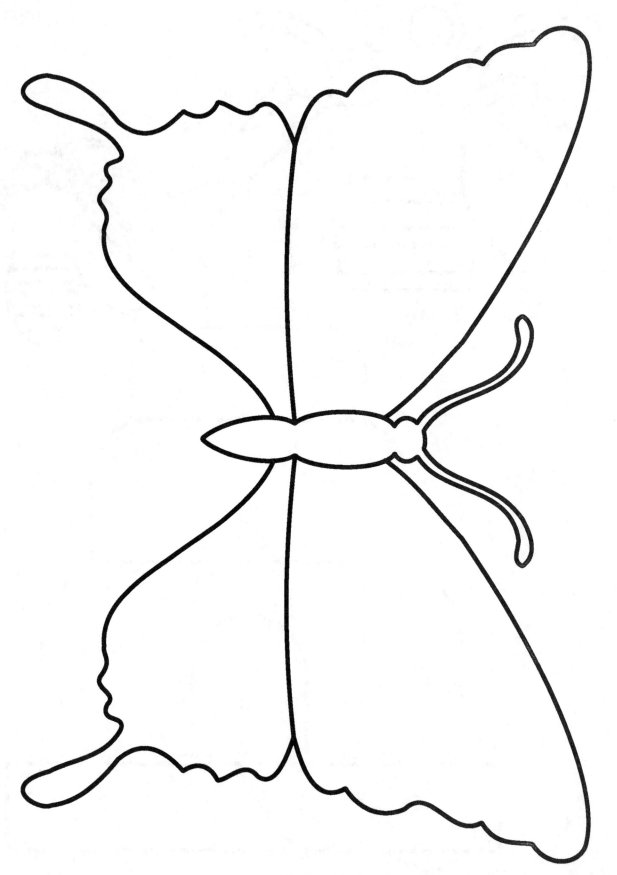

Butterfly
Life Cycle

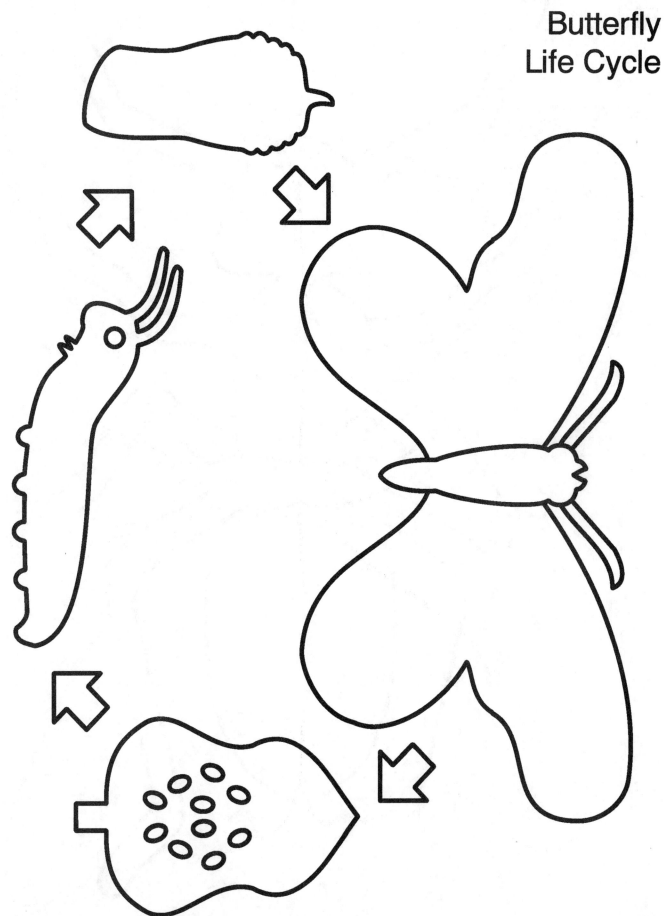

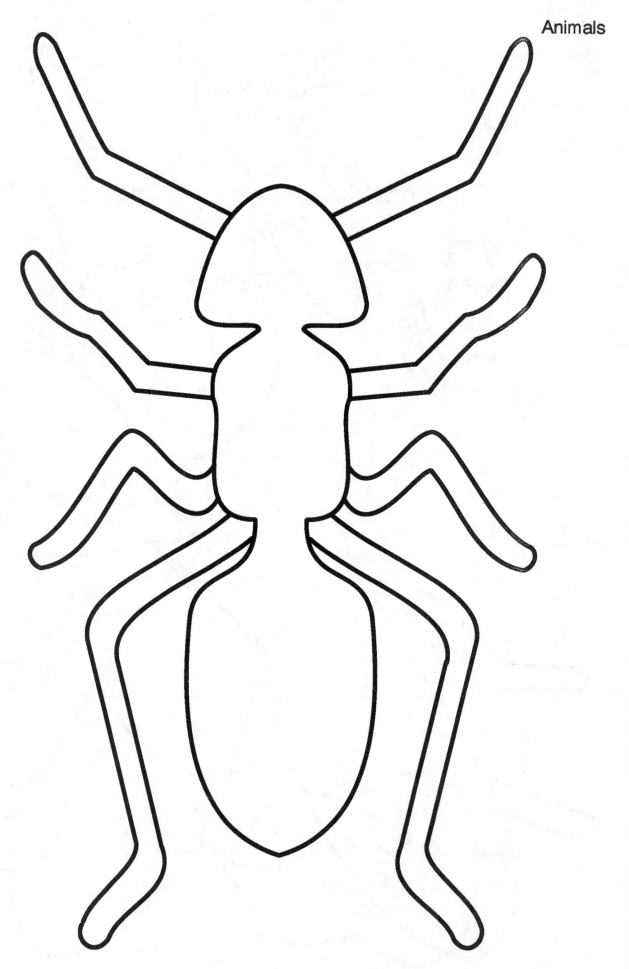

Fly

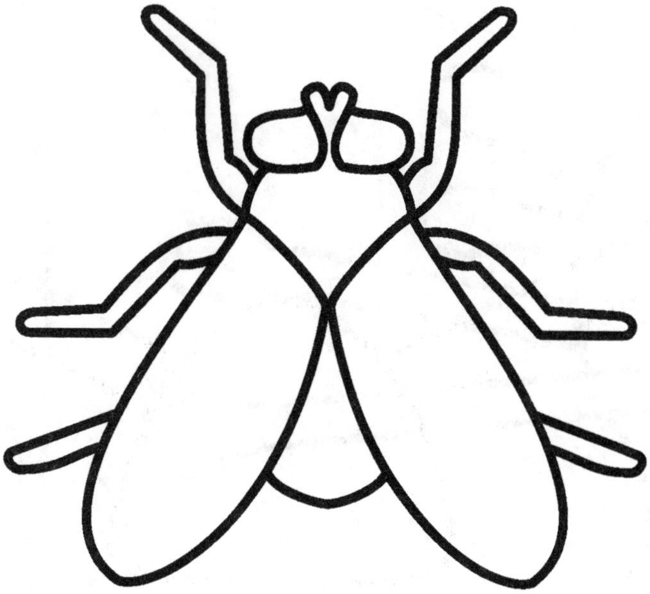

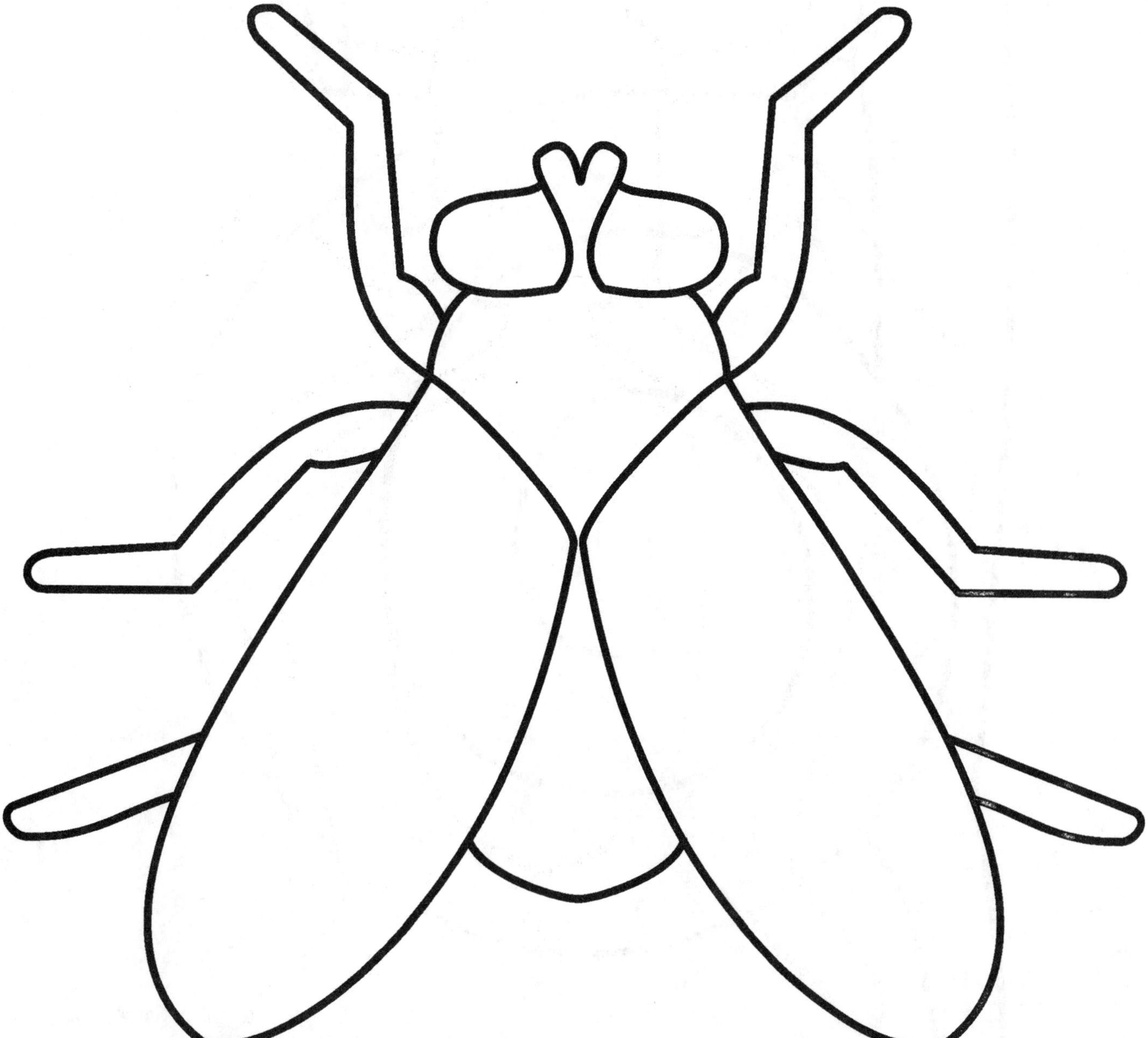

Snail

Brontosaurus

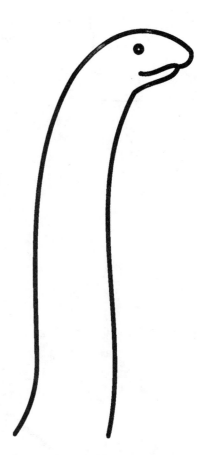

Attach this section to body.

Finished pattern will look like the above.

Stegosaurus

Triceratops

Tyrannosaurus

Pedestrian Sign

Stop Sign

The Giant Book of Theme Patterns © 1993 Fearon Teacher Aids

Traffic Signal

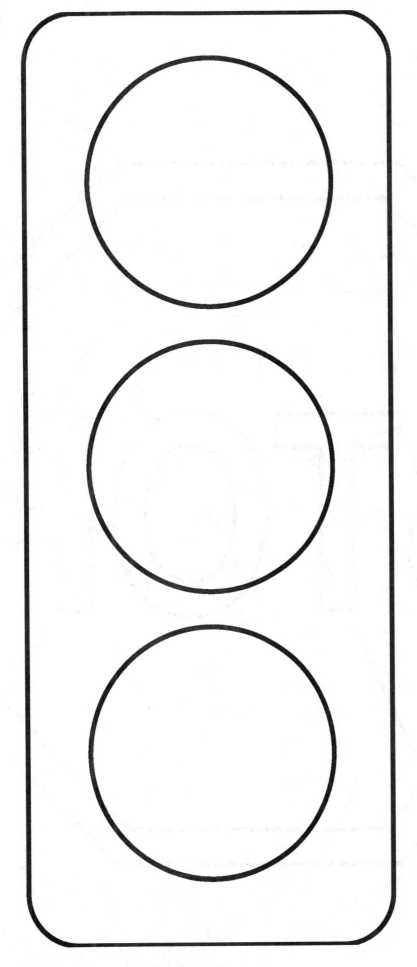

Airplane

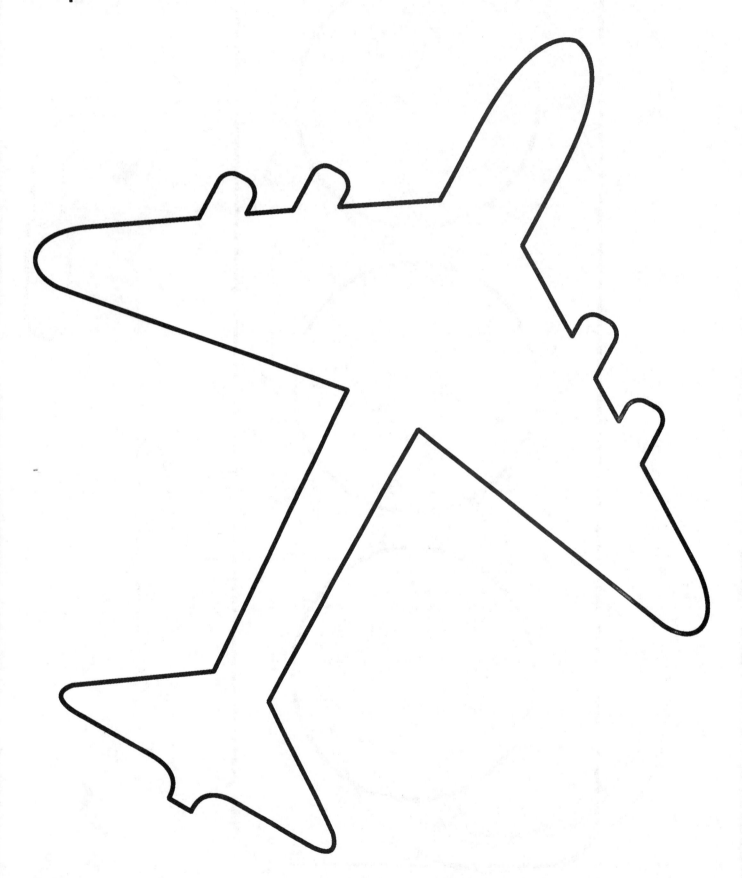

Bicycle

Bus

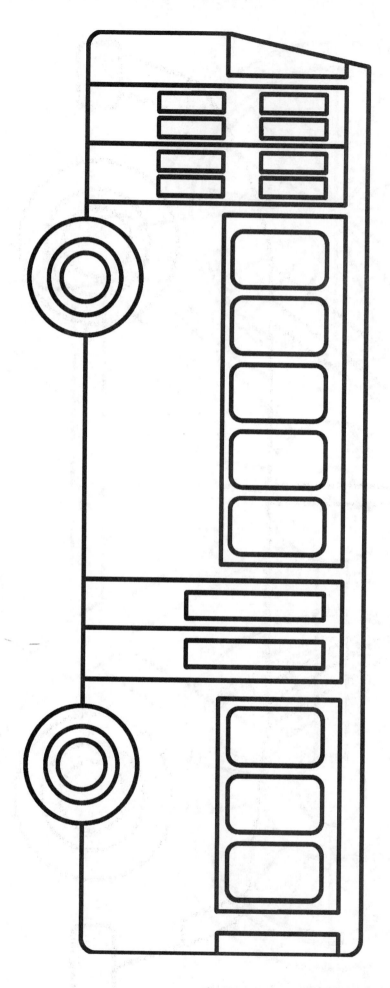

Car

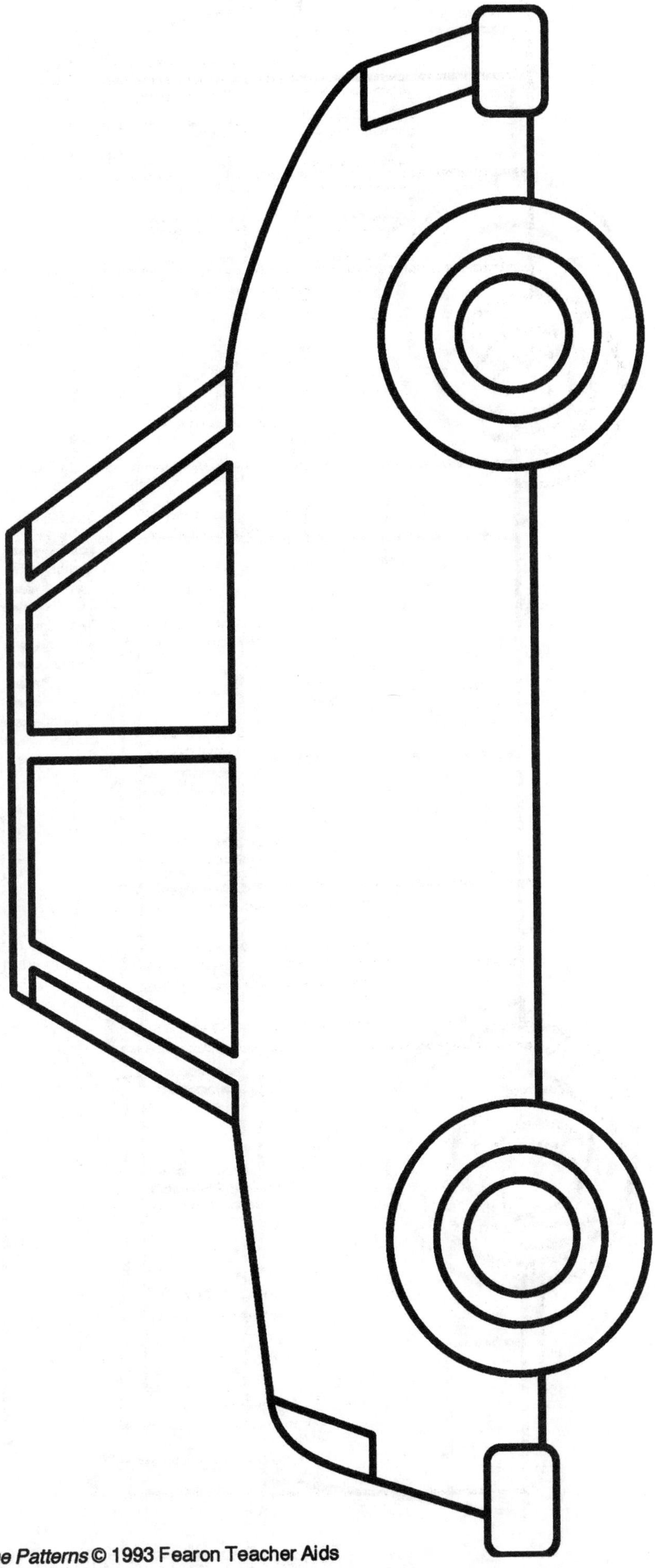

Fire Truck

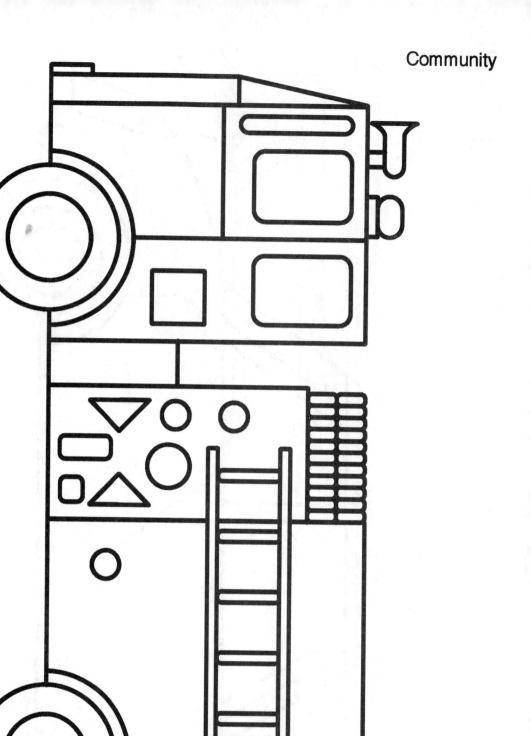

Helicopter

Attach rotary
blade here.

Finished helicopter will
look like the above.

Jeep

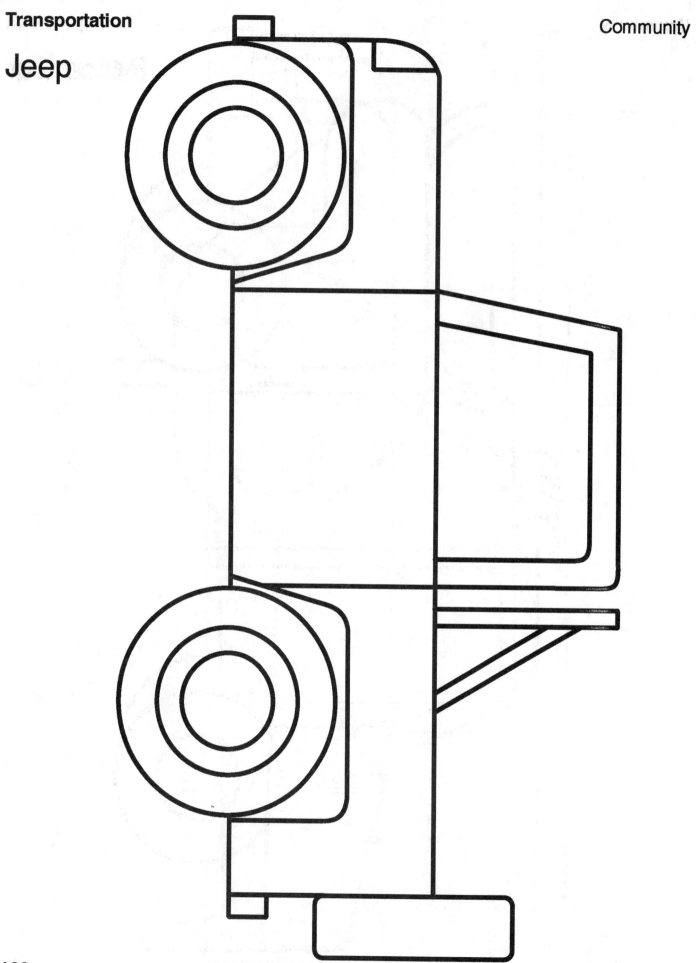

Police Car

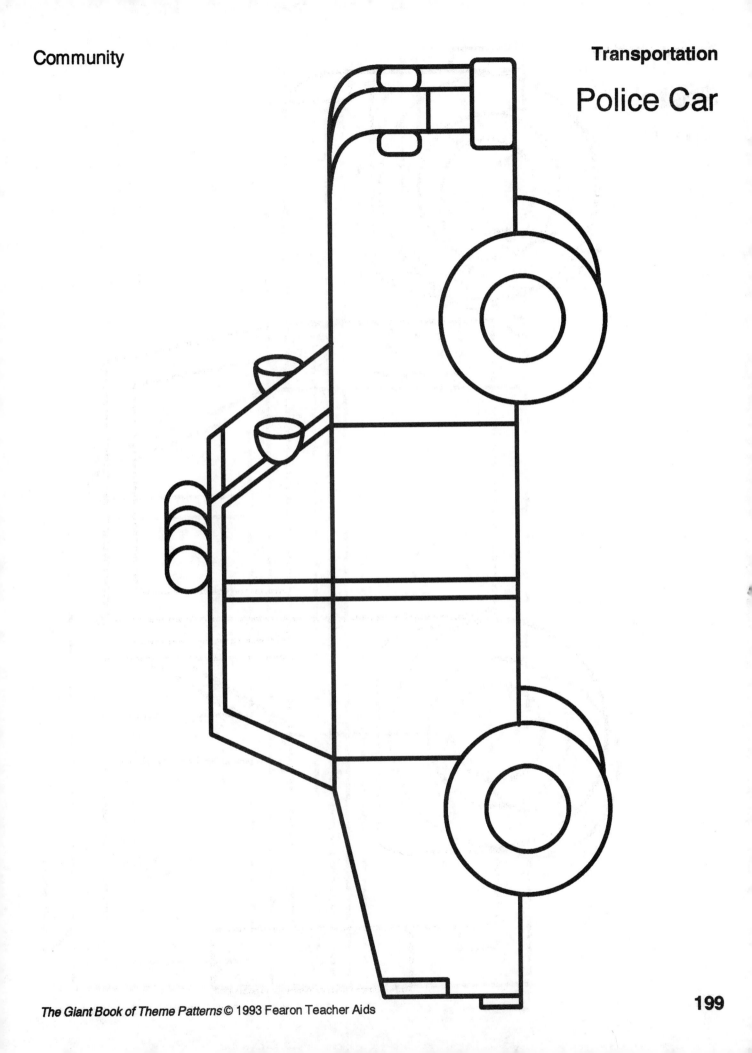

Postal
Truck

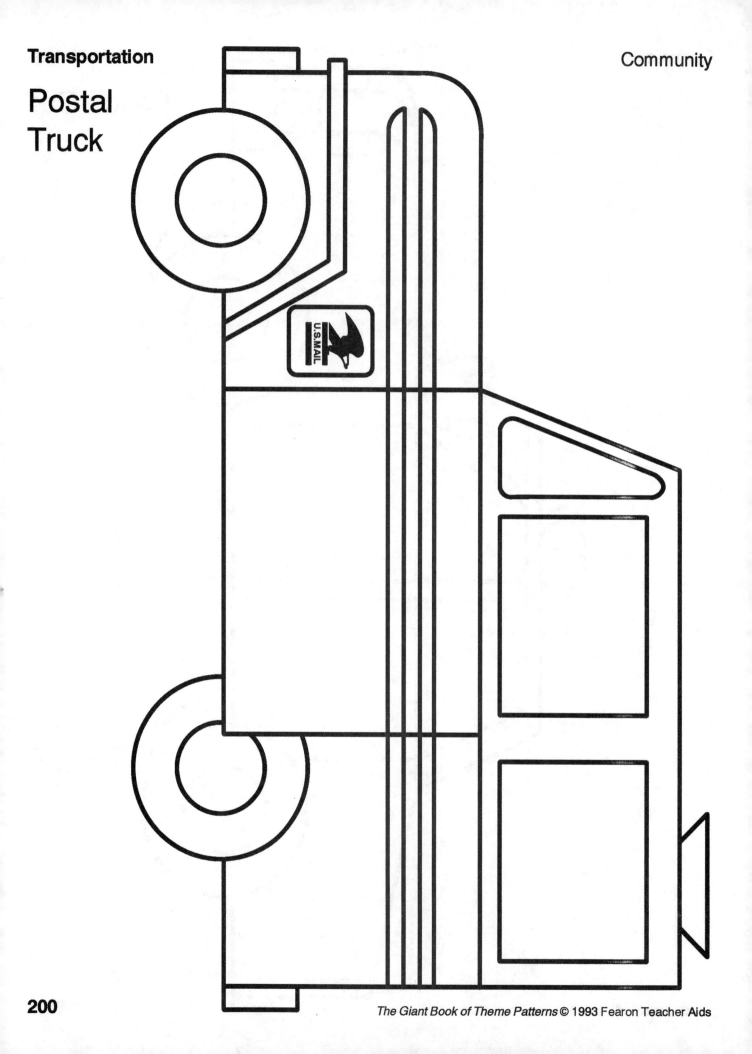

U.S.MAIL

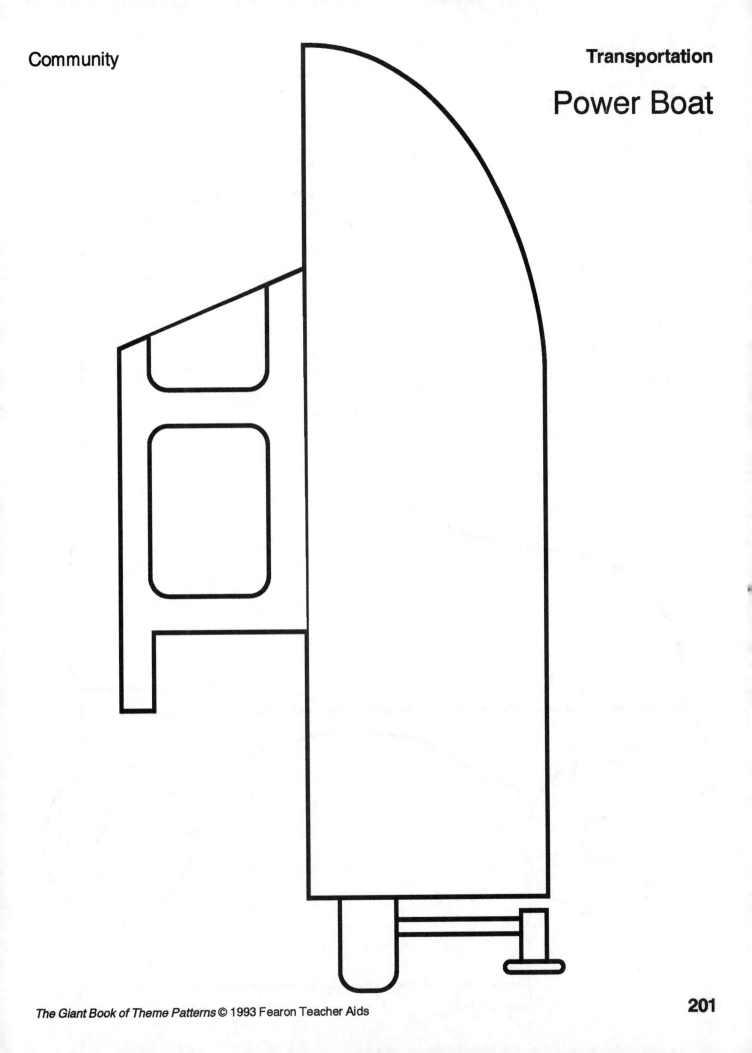

Roller Skate

Sailboat

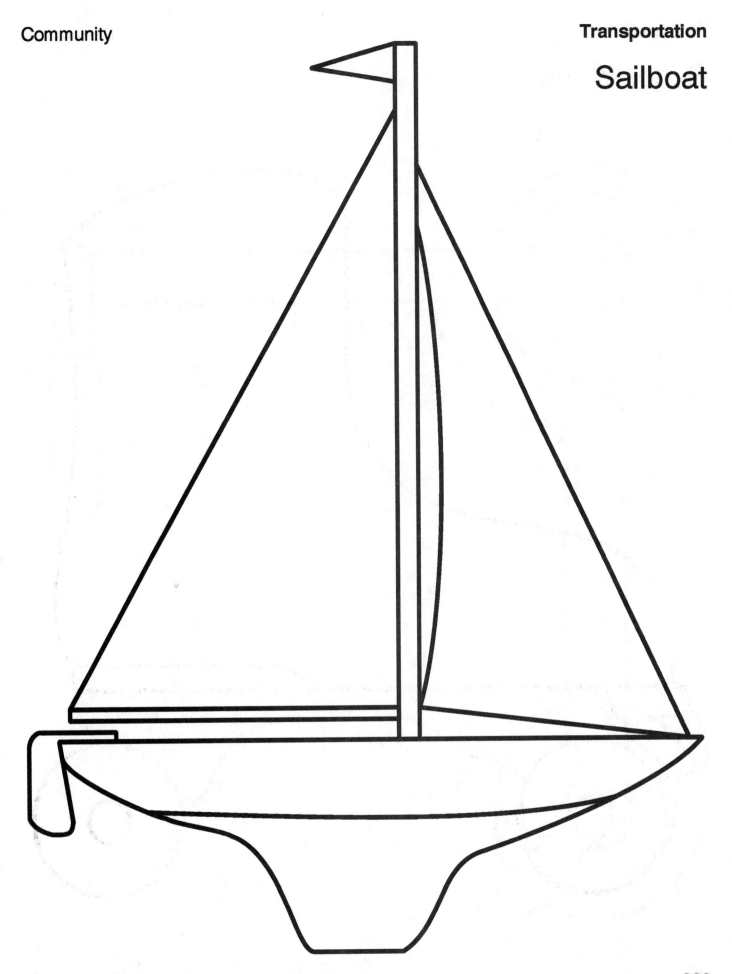

Scooter

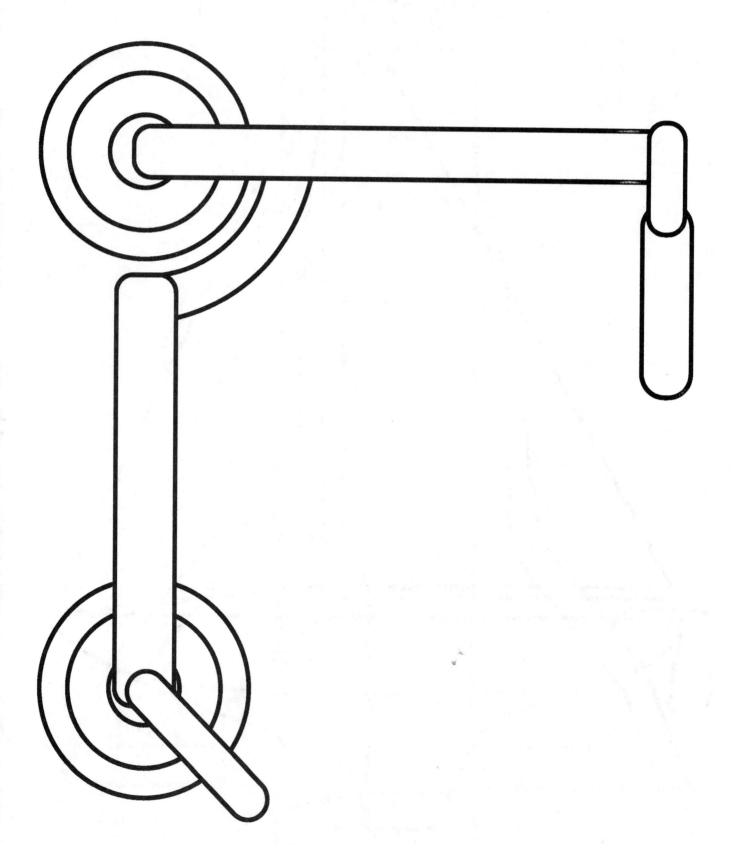

Space Shuttle

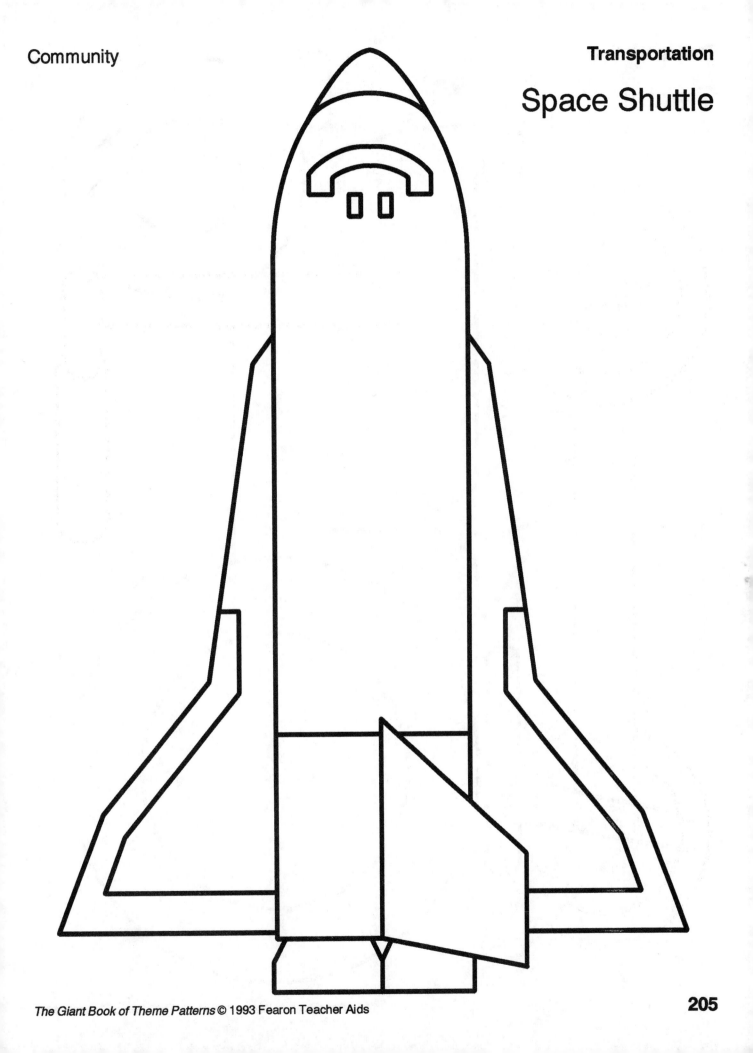

Tractor

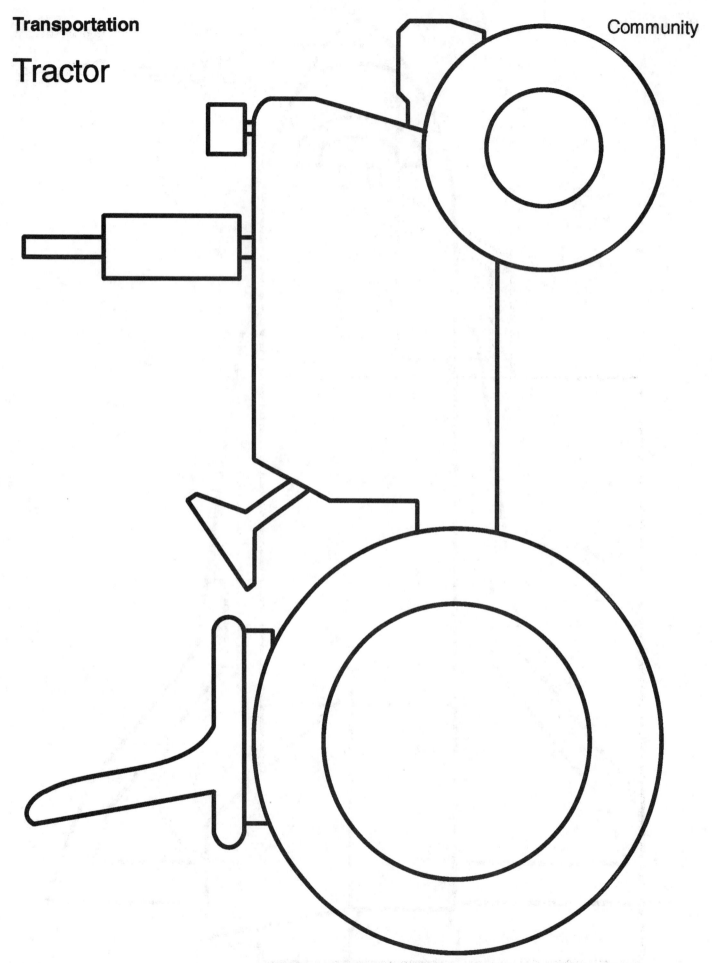

Truck

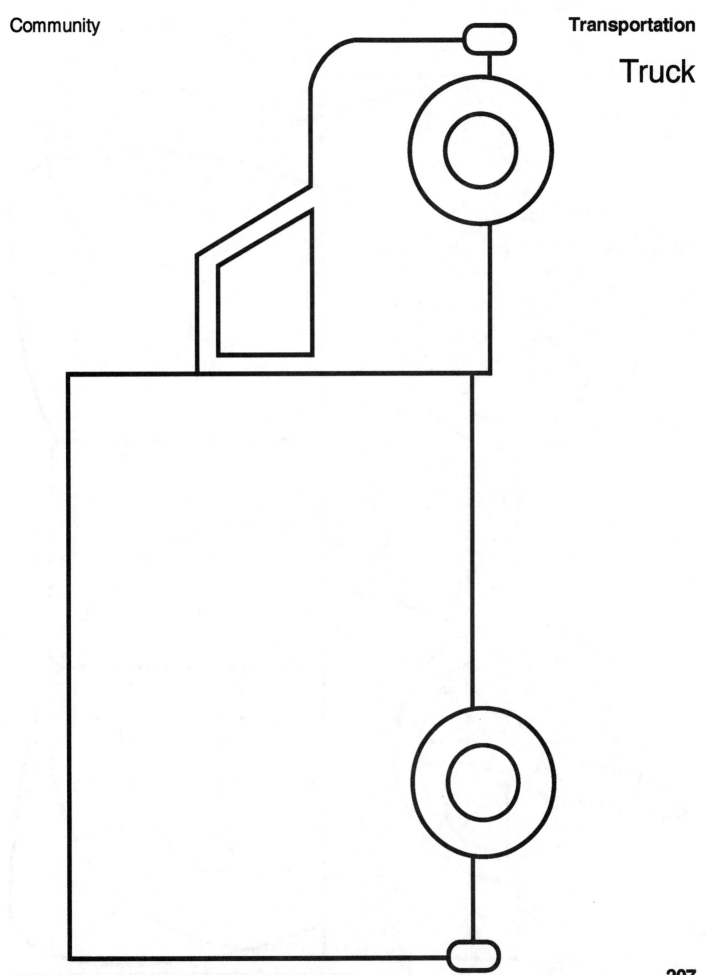

Covered Wagon

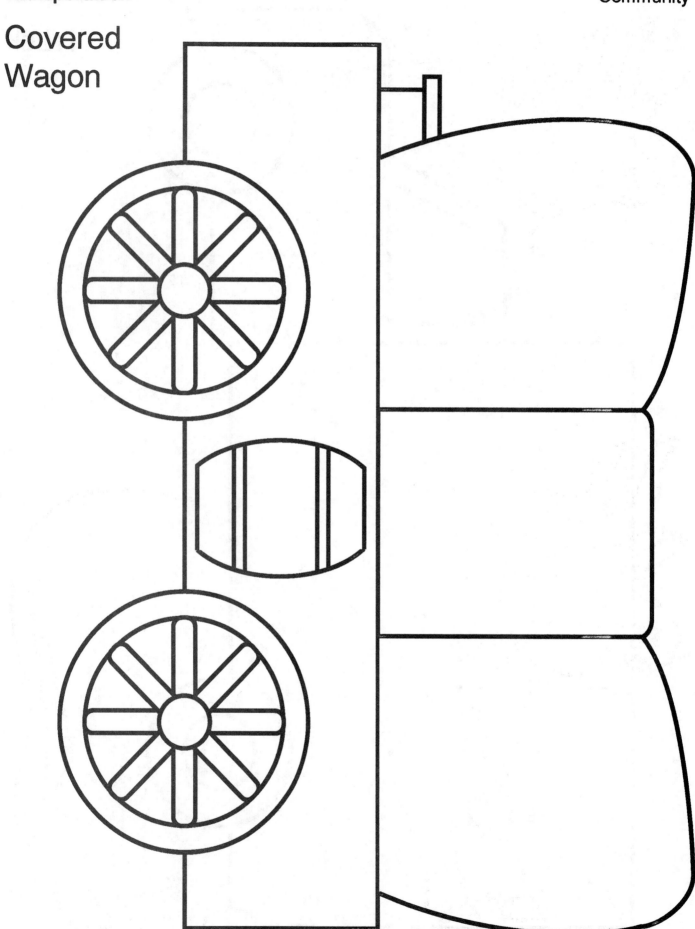

Use this ox with covered wagon.

Oxen

Astronaut

Crossing Guard

Firefighter

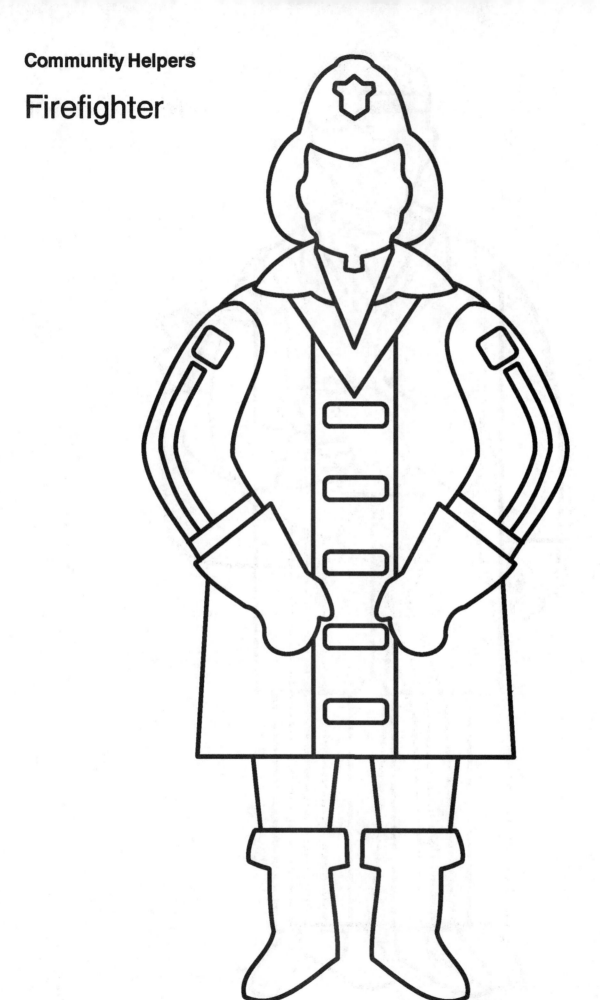

Mailbox

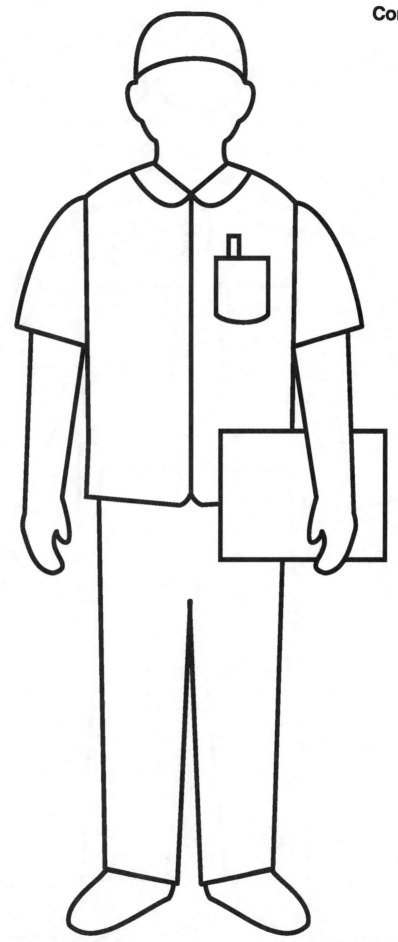

Police Officer

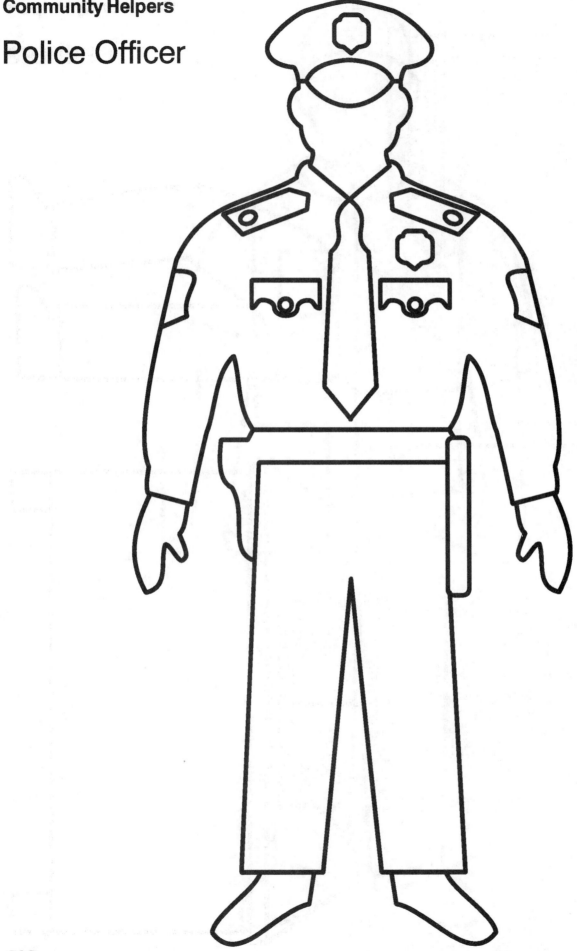

Teachers

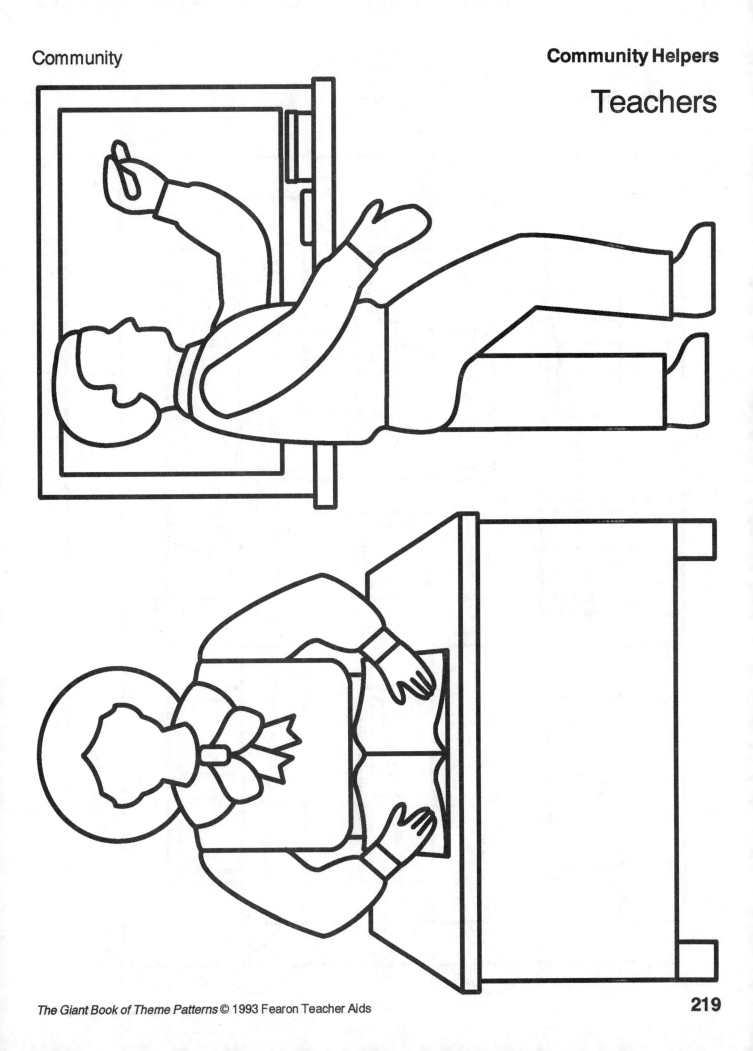

Apartment

The Giant Book of Theme Patterns © 1993 Fearon Teacher Aids

Bed, Pillow, and Quilt

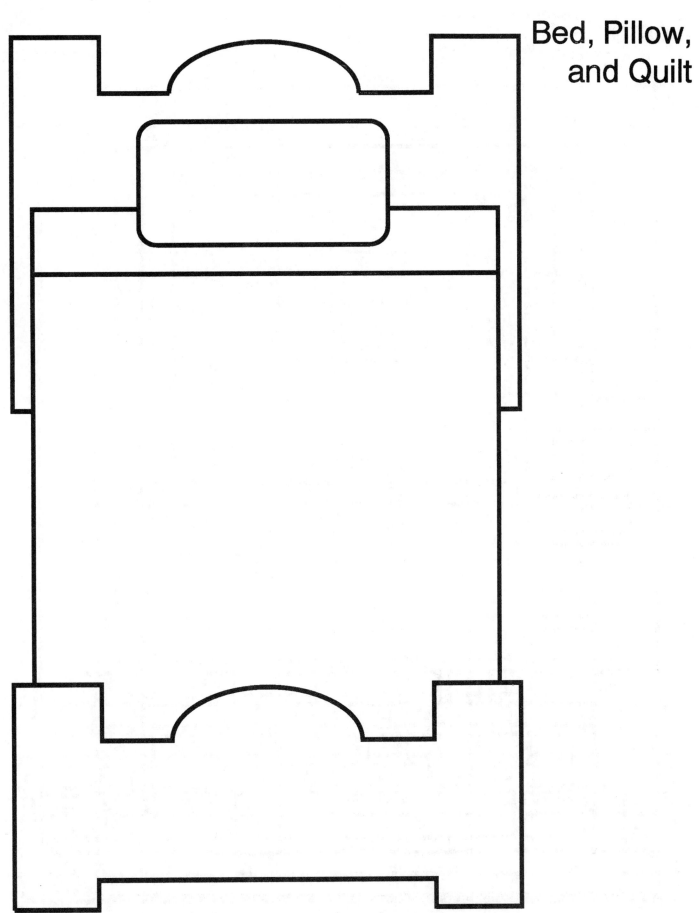

Computer

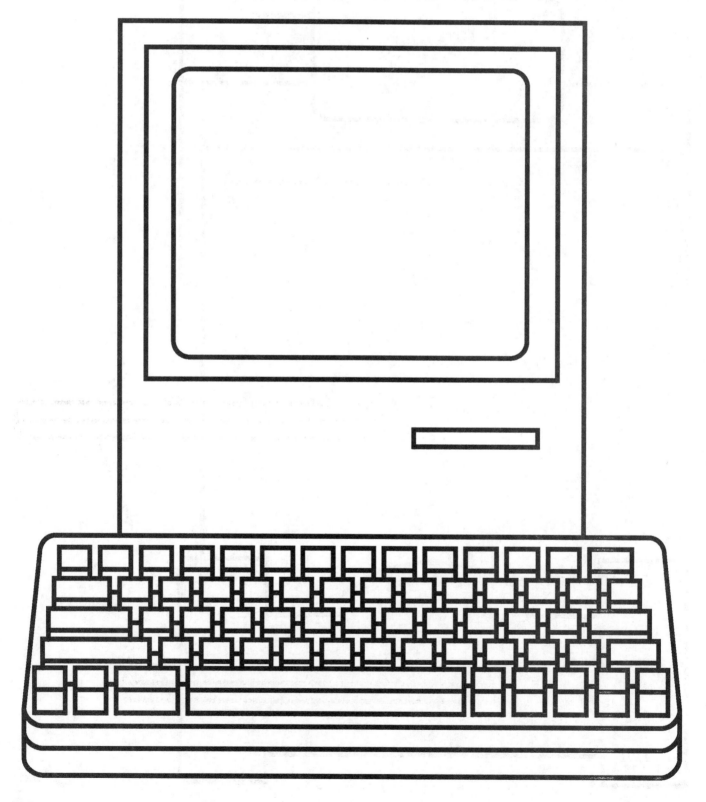

Desk

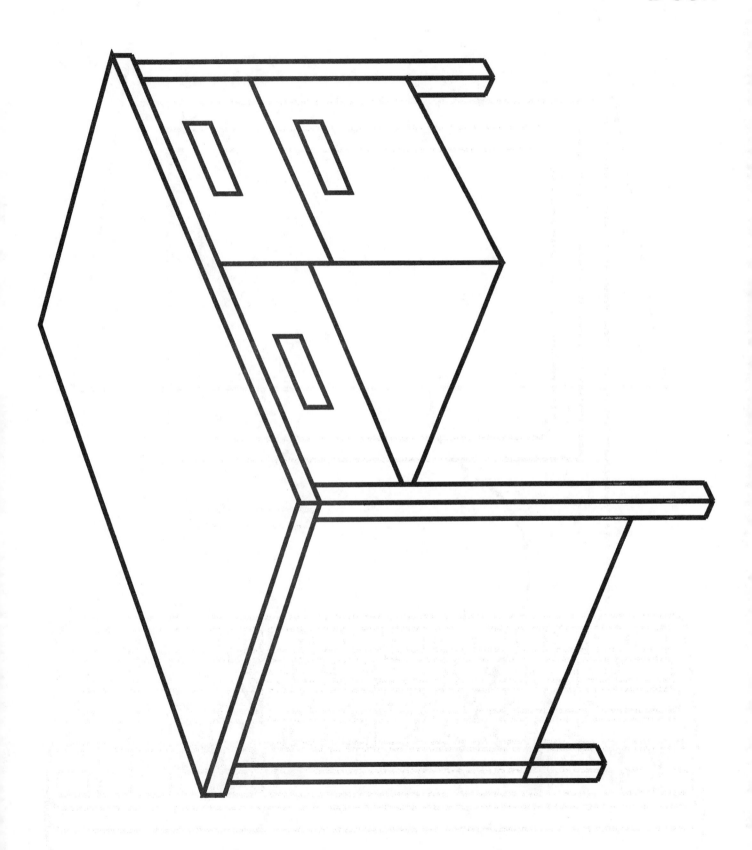

Lamp

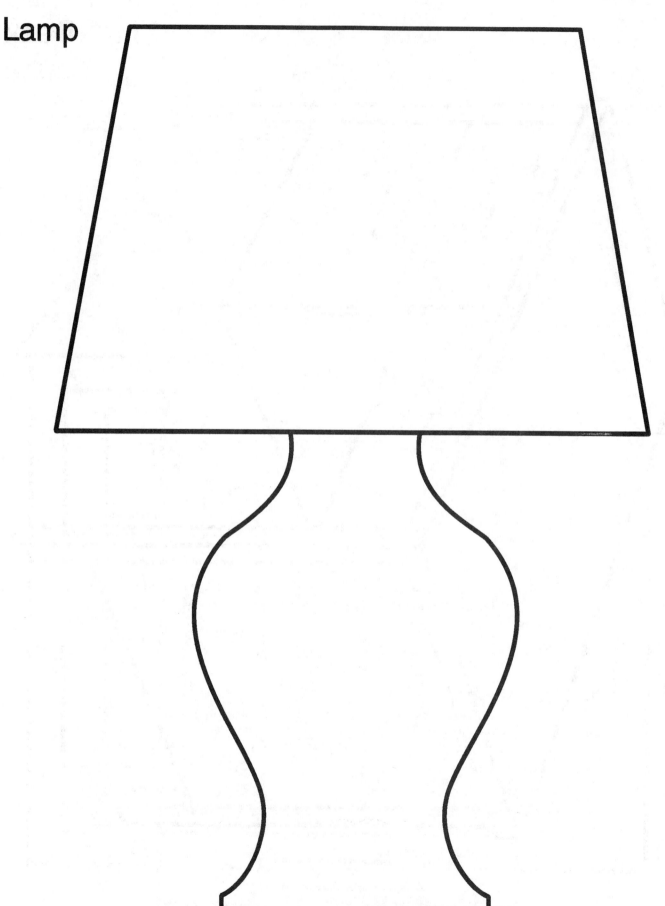

Lawn Mower

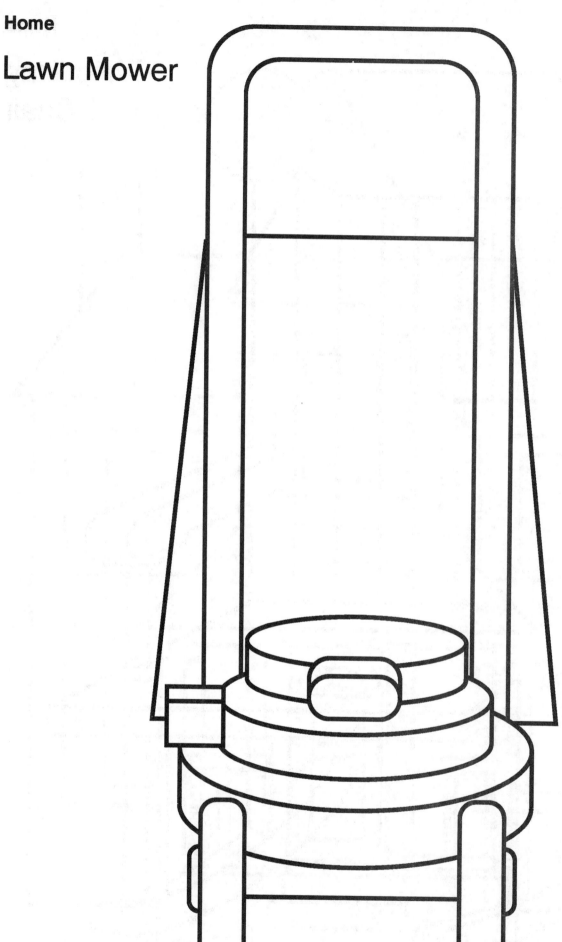

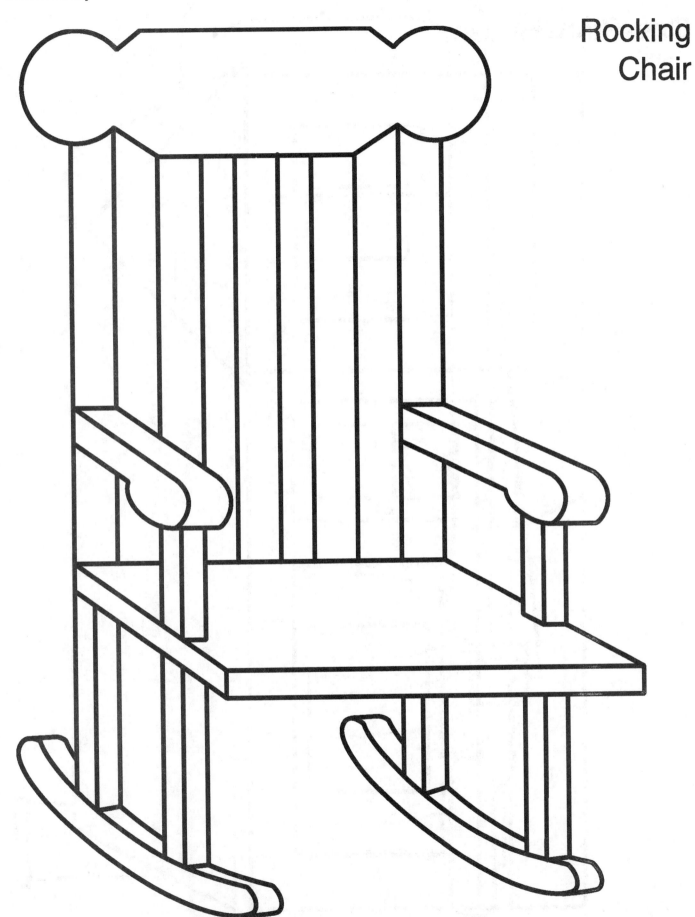

One-Story House

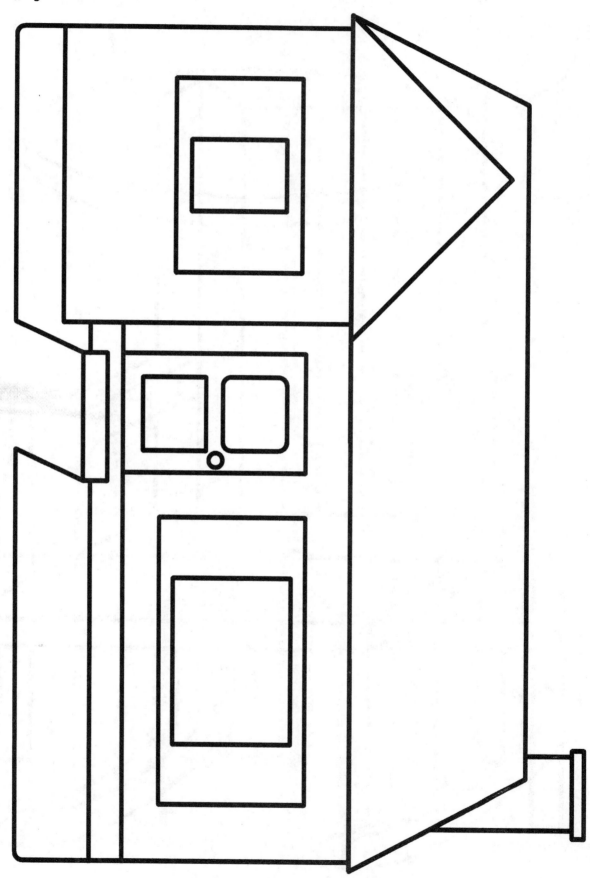

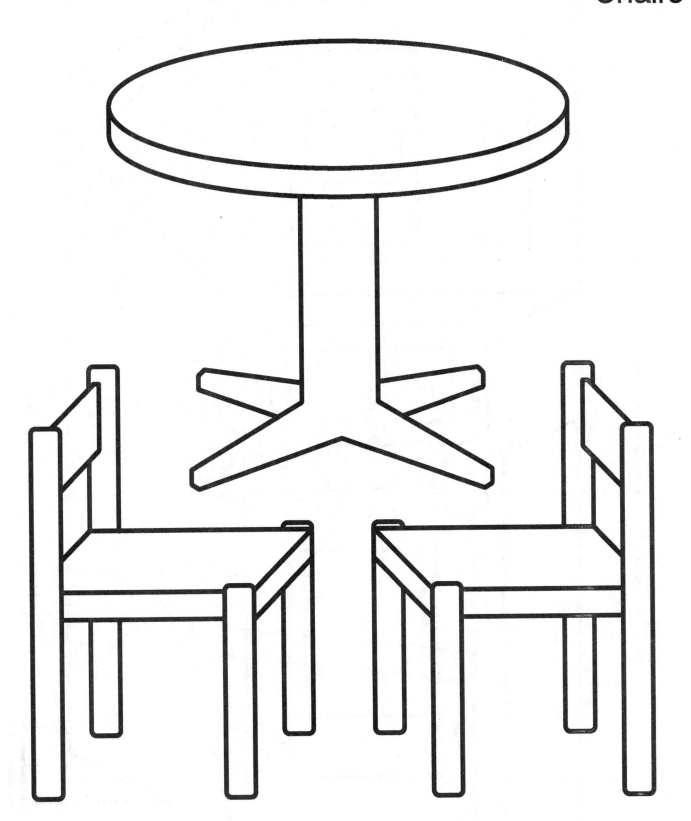

Telephone

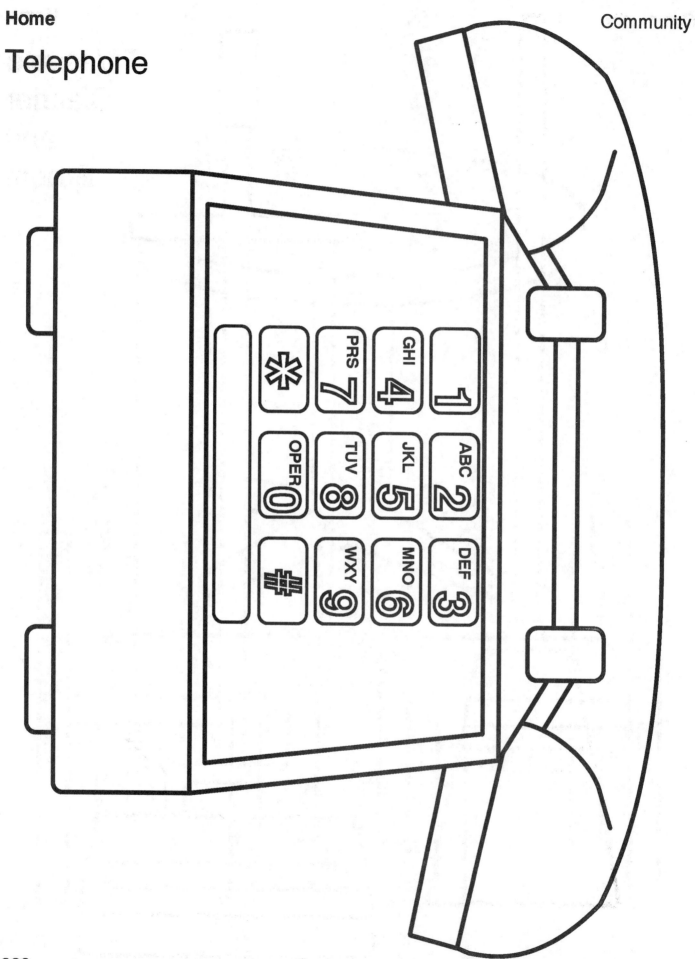

Vacuum Cleaner and Broom

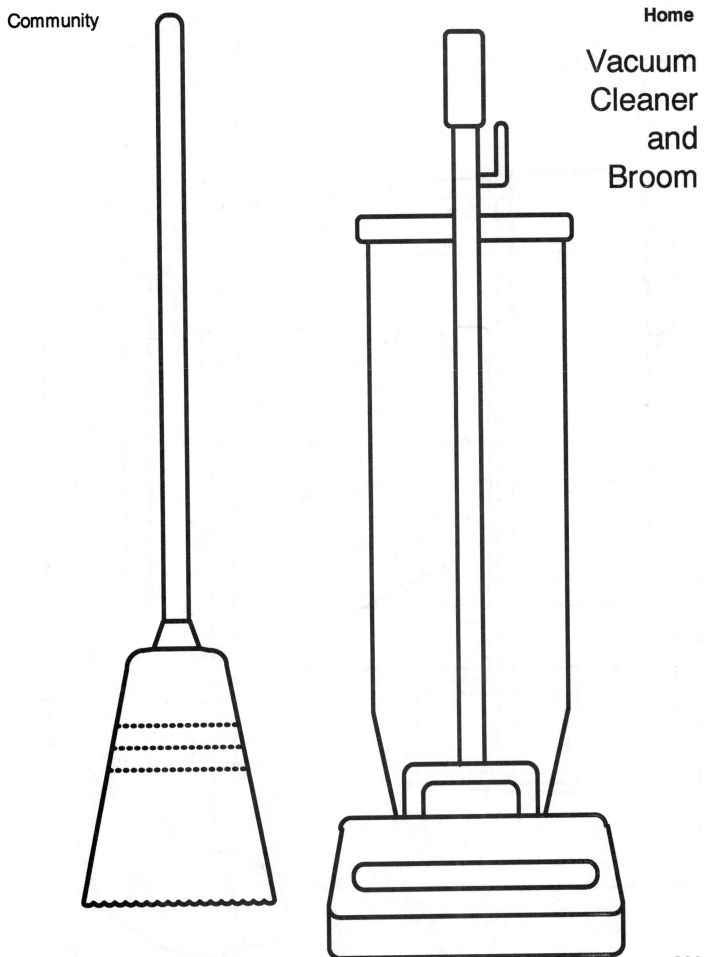

Backpack

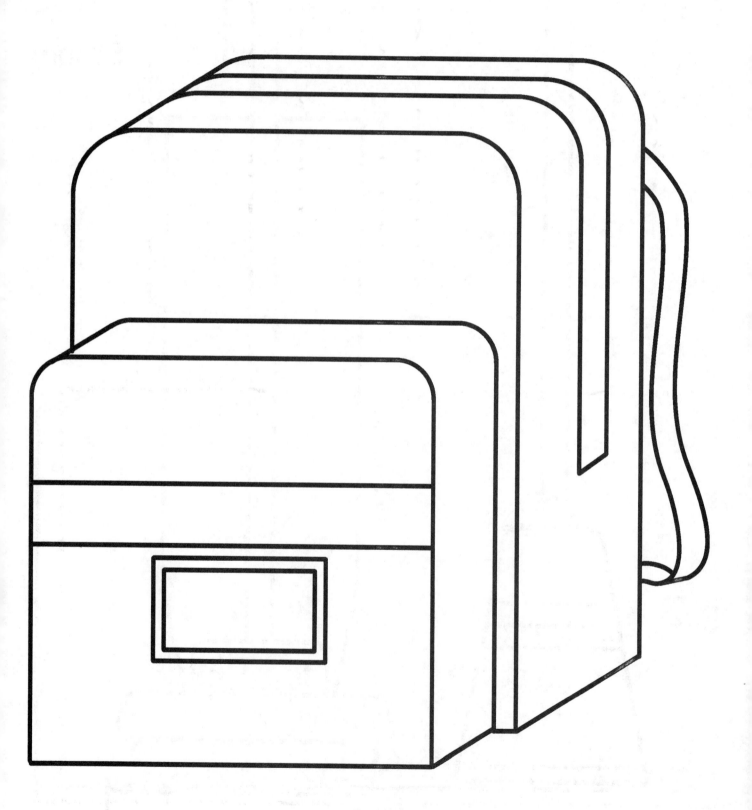

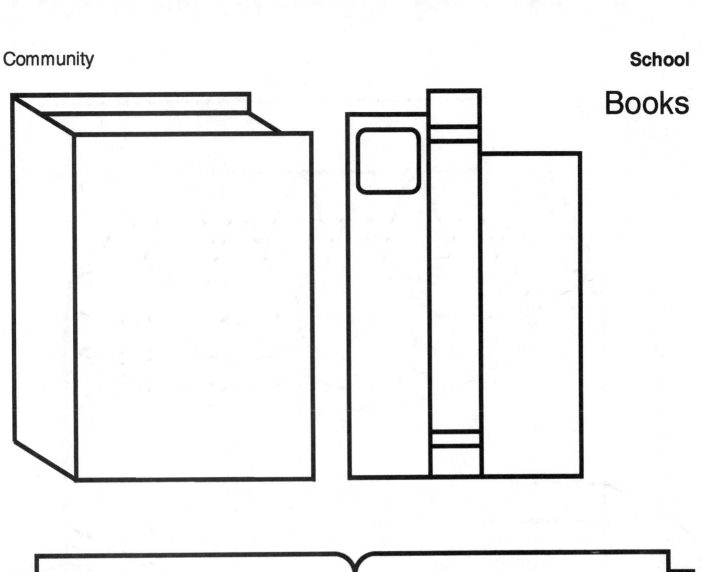

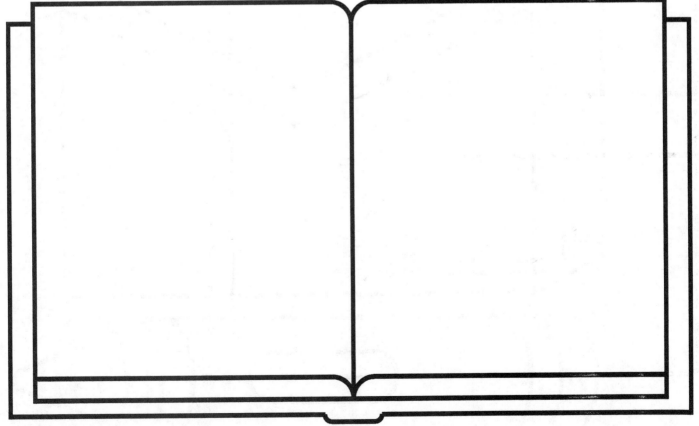

Crayons

Pad and Pencil

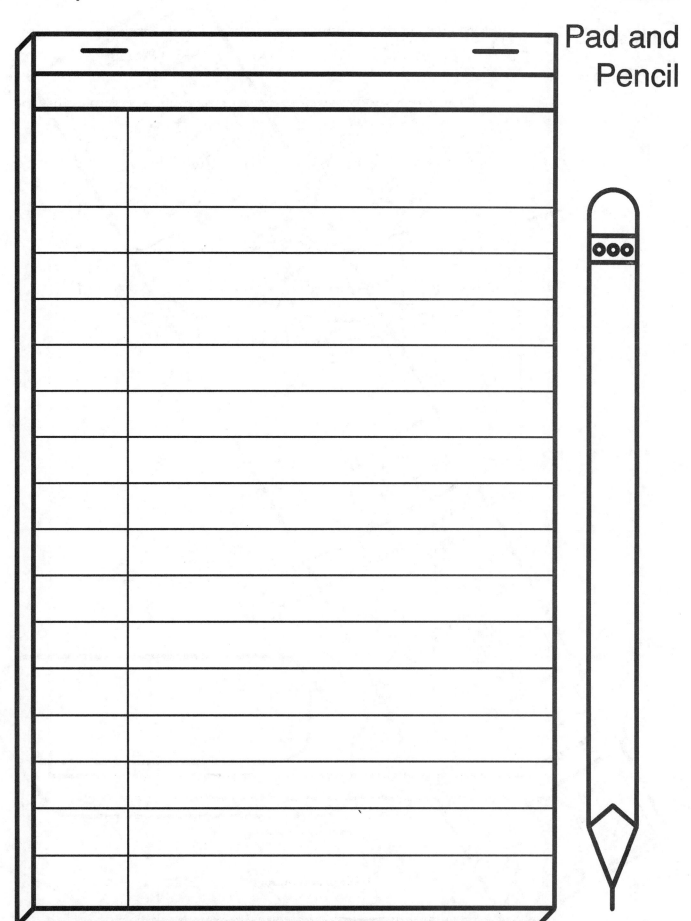

Ruler and Eraser

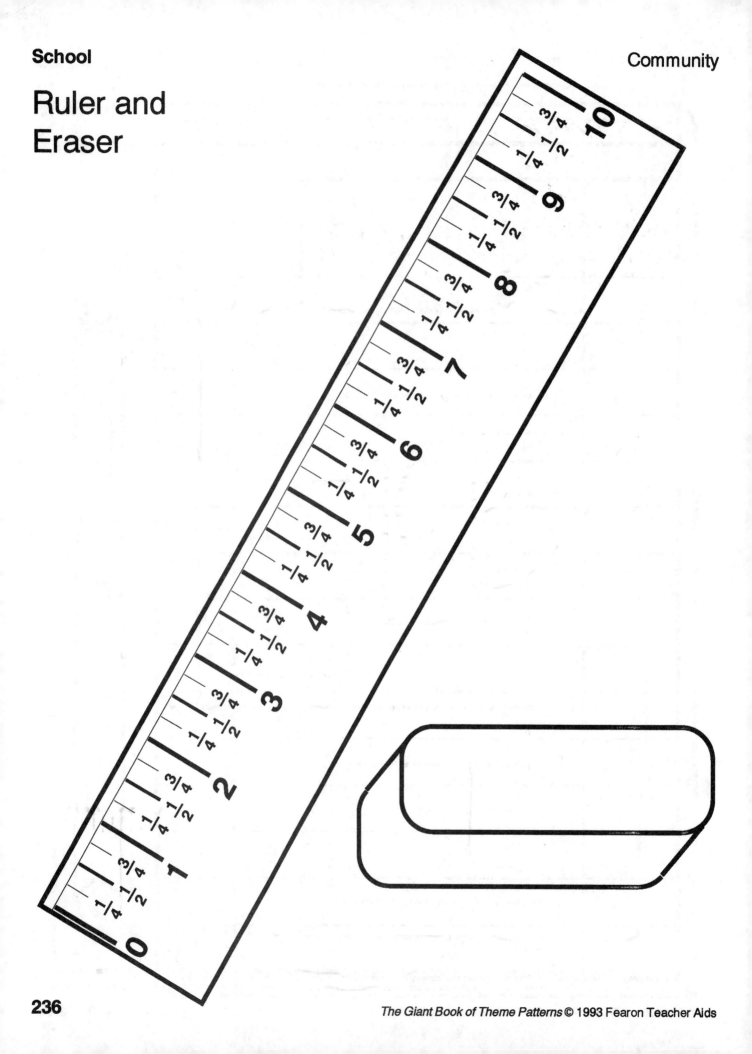

The Giant Book of Theme Patterns © 1993 Fearon Teacher Aids

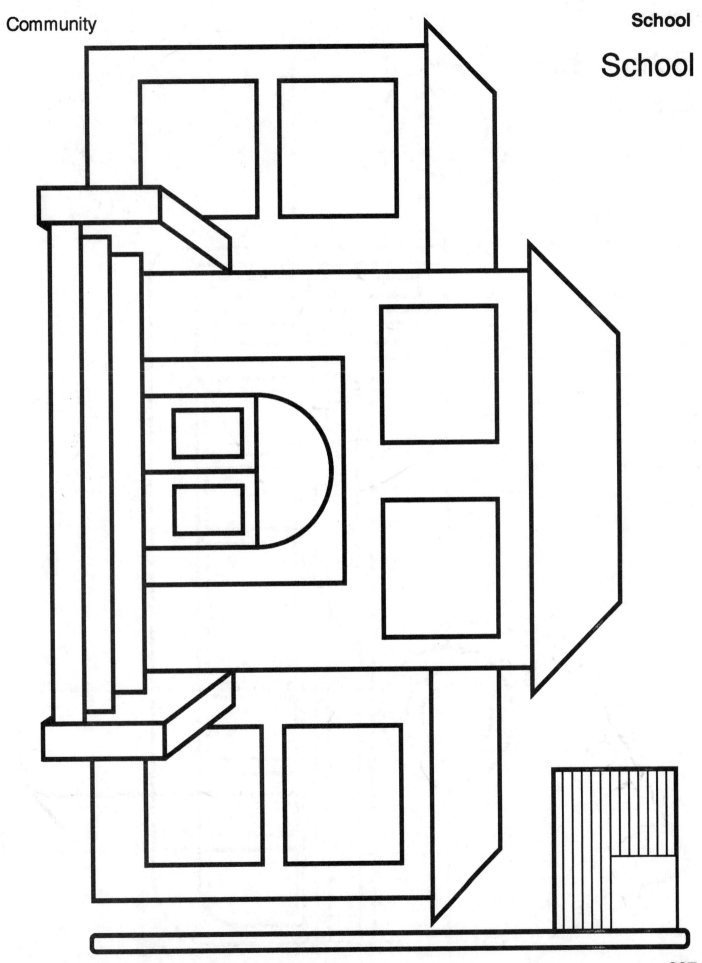

School Bus

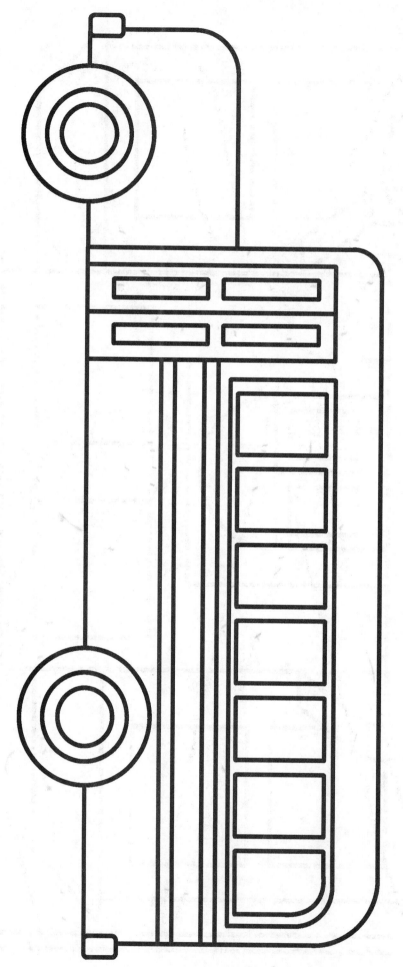

Scissors

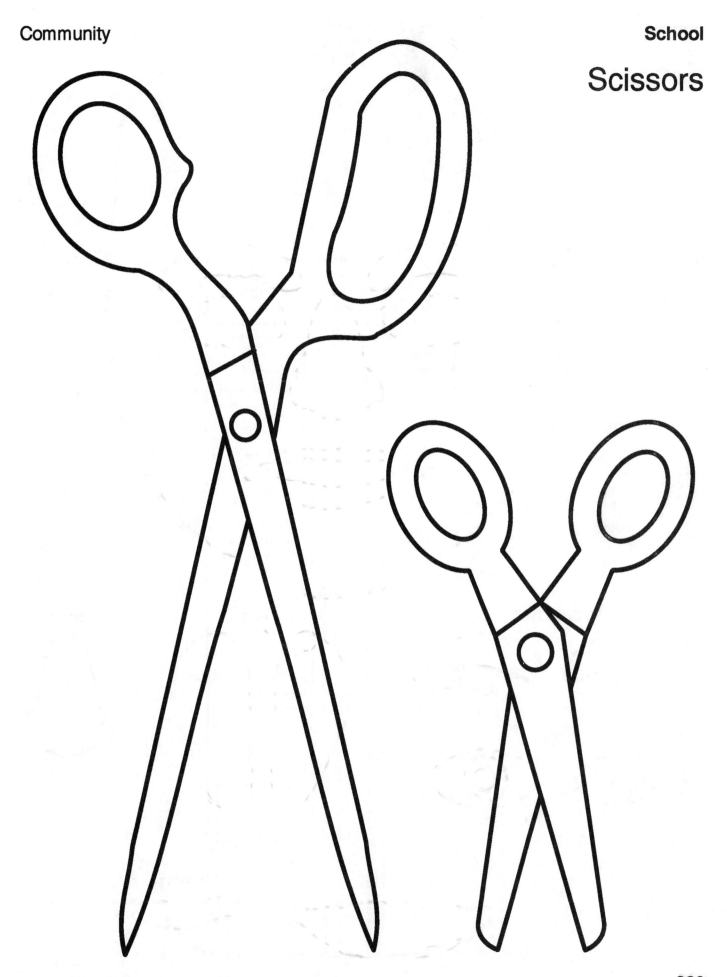

Face

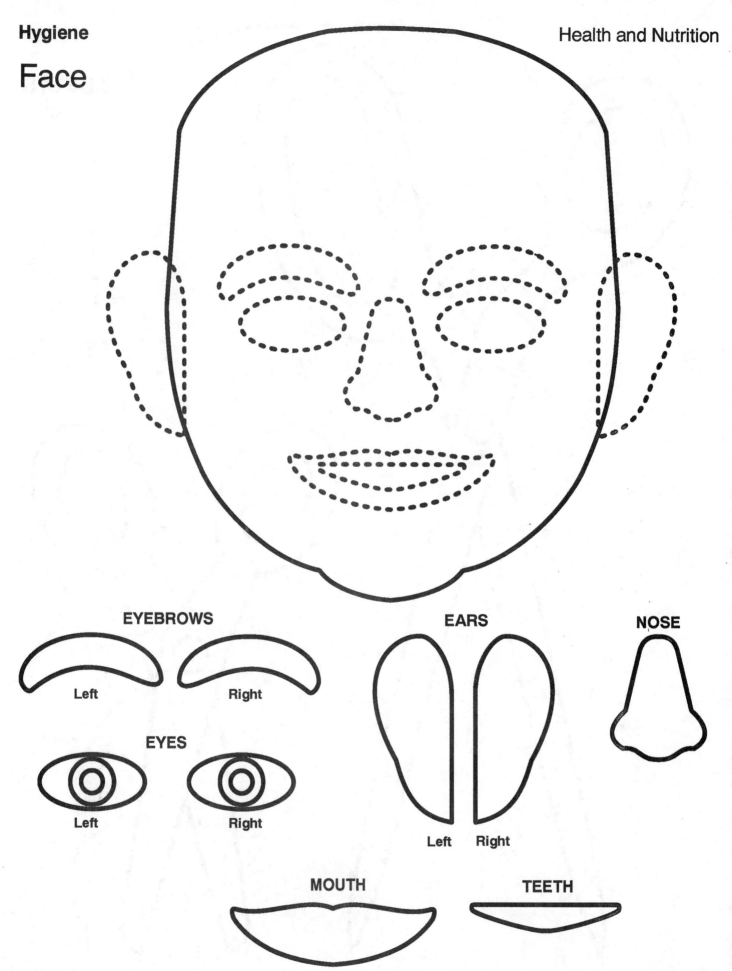

EYEBROWS

Left

Right

EARS

NOSE

EYES

Left

Right

Left   Right

MOUTH

TEETH

Hair

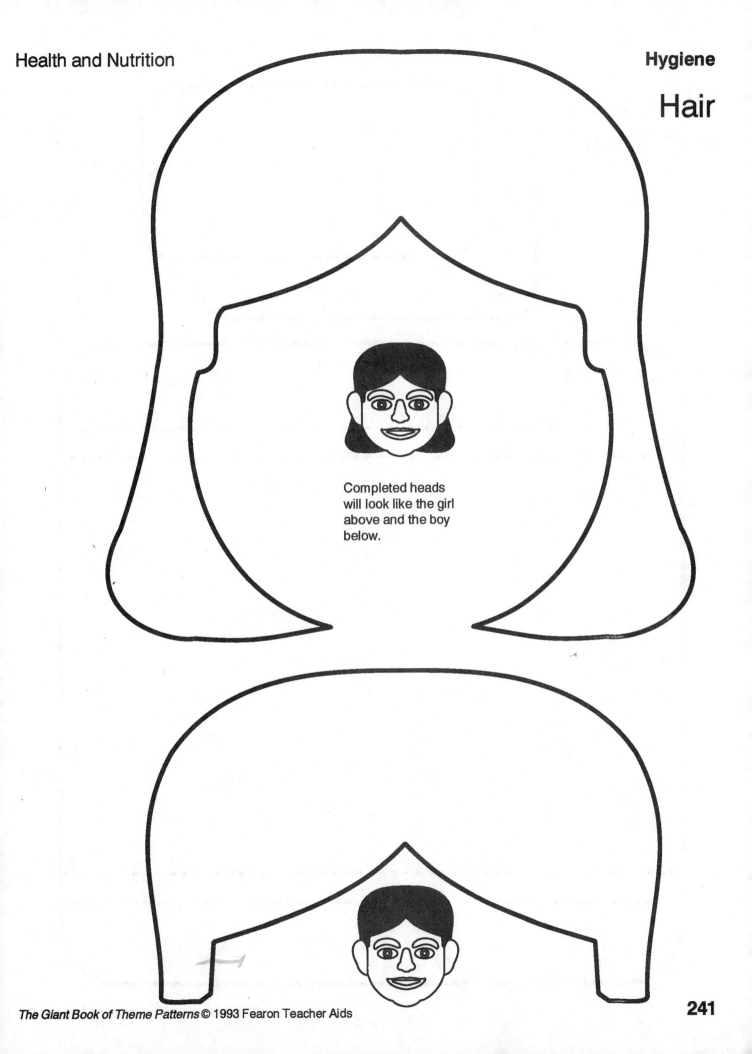

Completed heads
will look like the girl
above and the boy
below.

Washcloth
and Soap

Toothpaste
and
Toothbrush

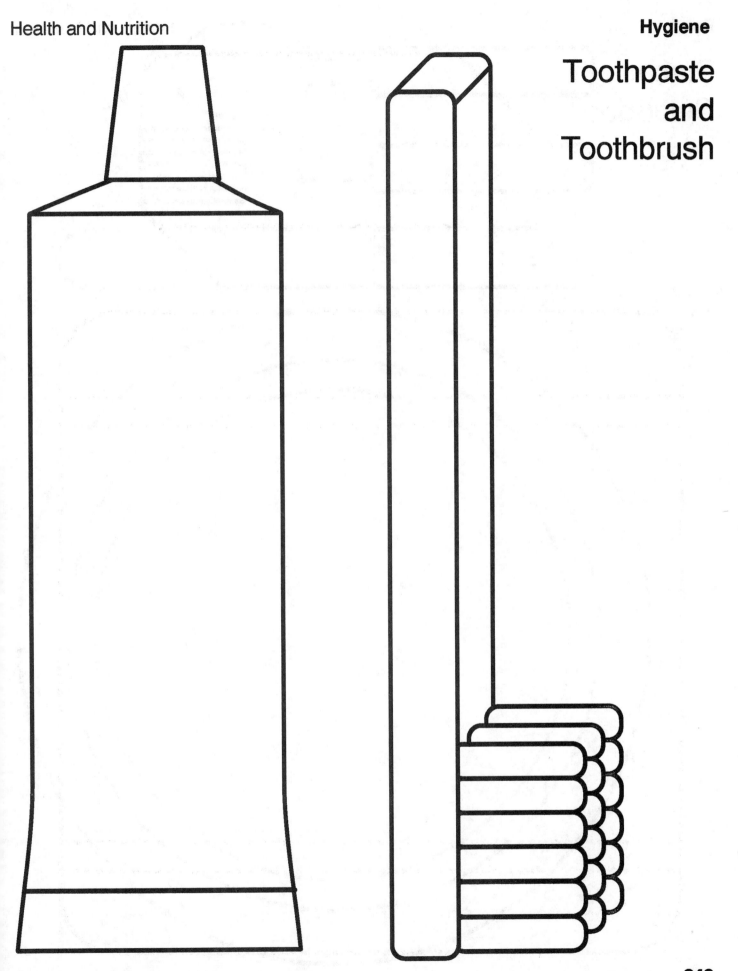

Place Setting

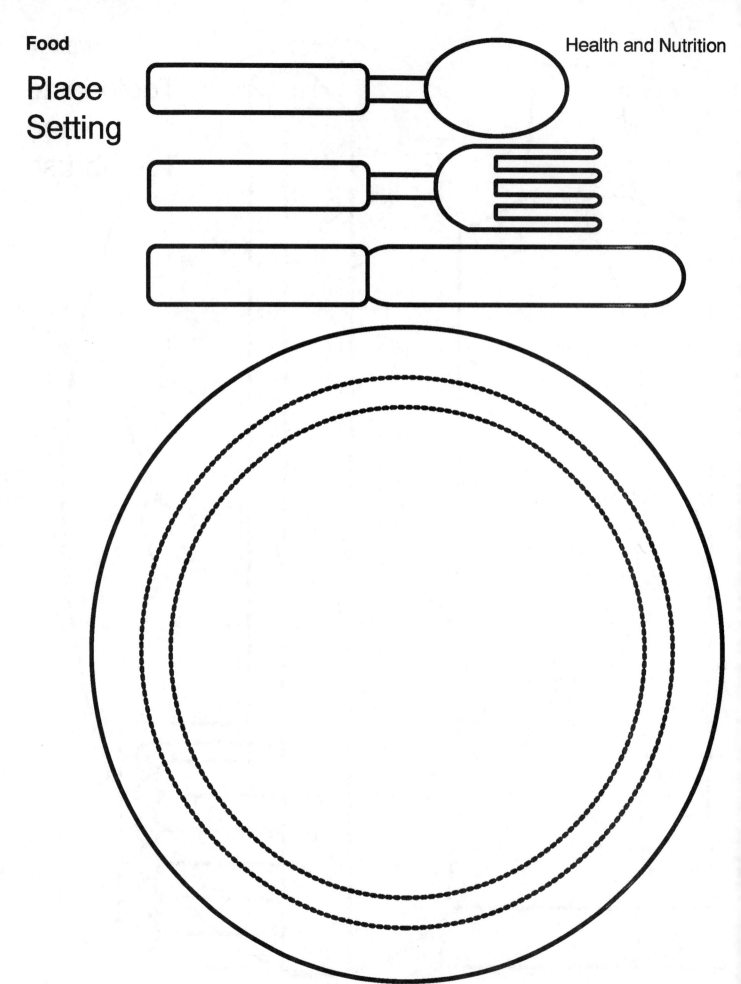

Beef
Dinner

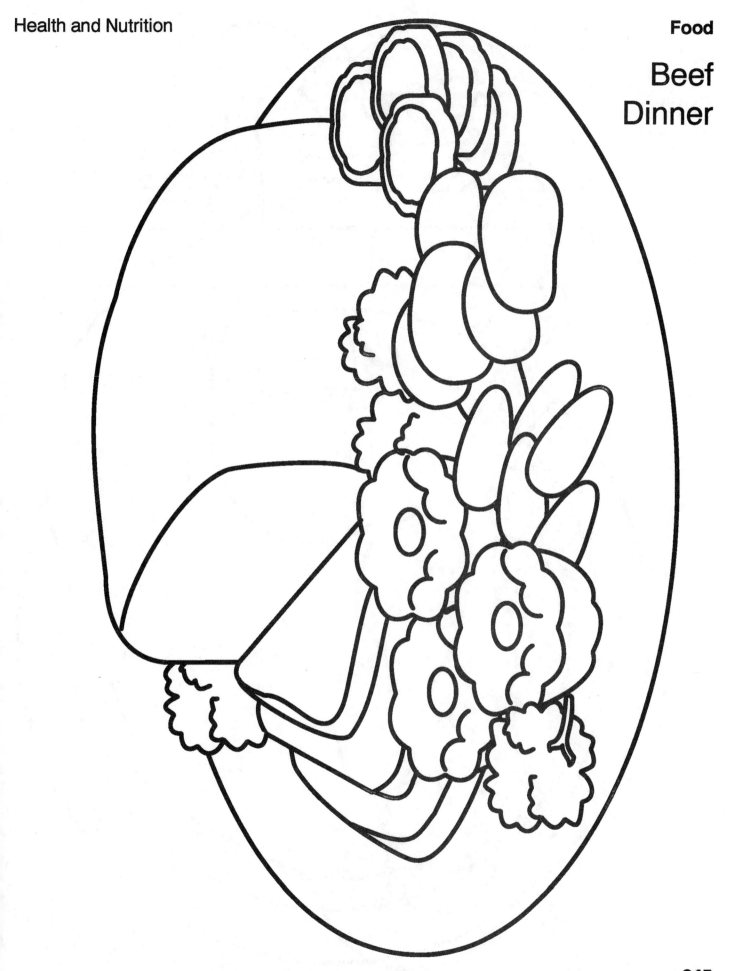

Turkey
Dinner

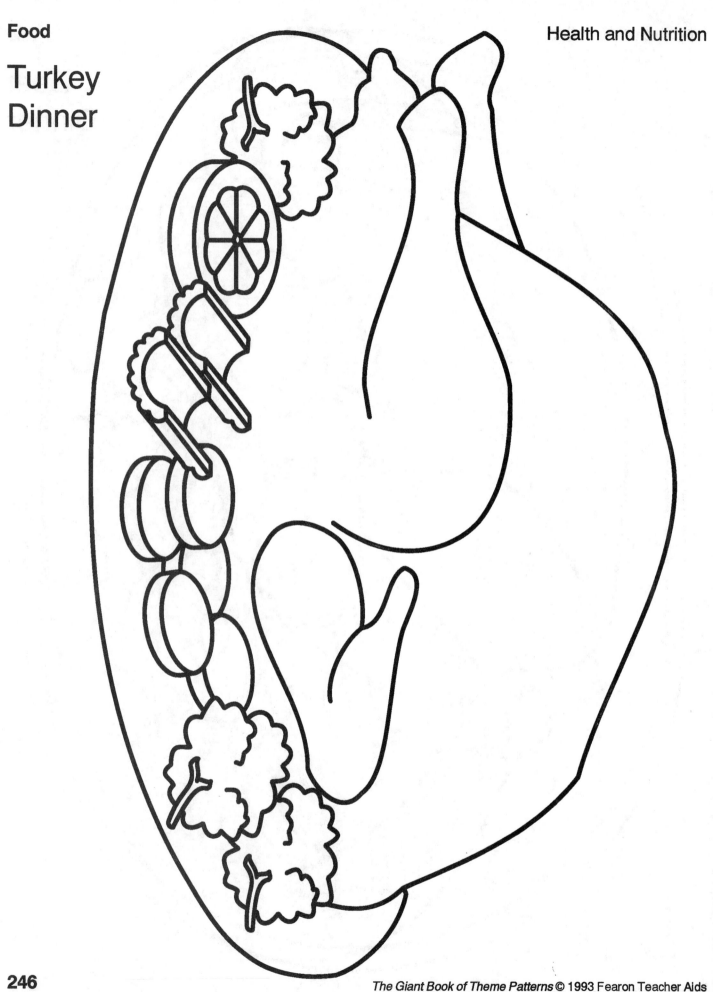

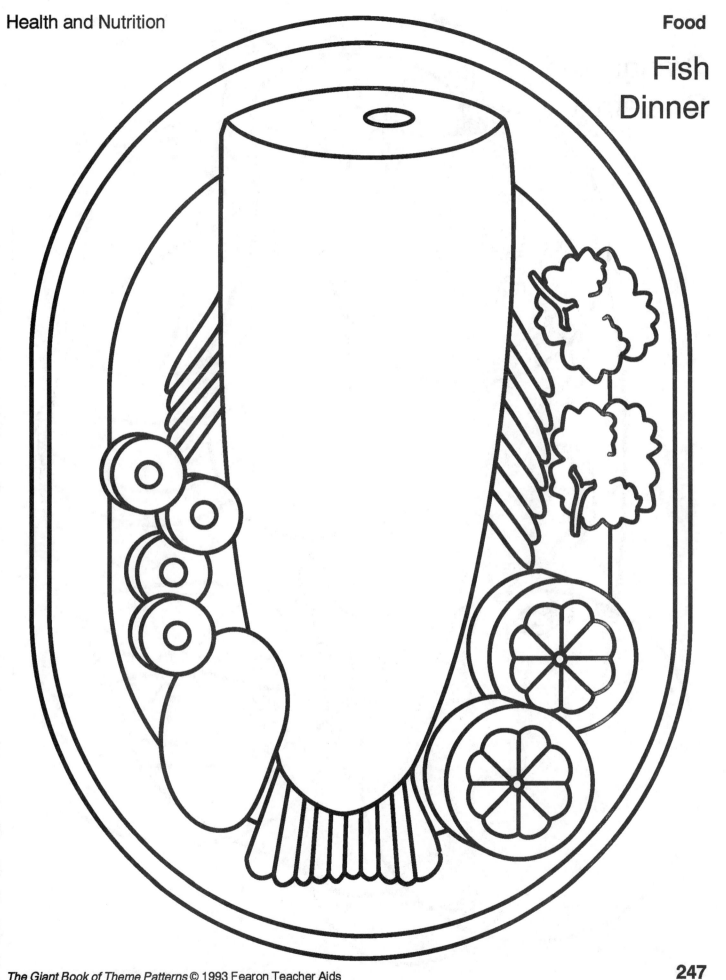

Orange and Grapefruit

Lemon and Apple

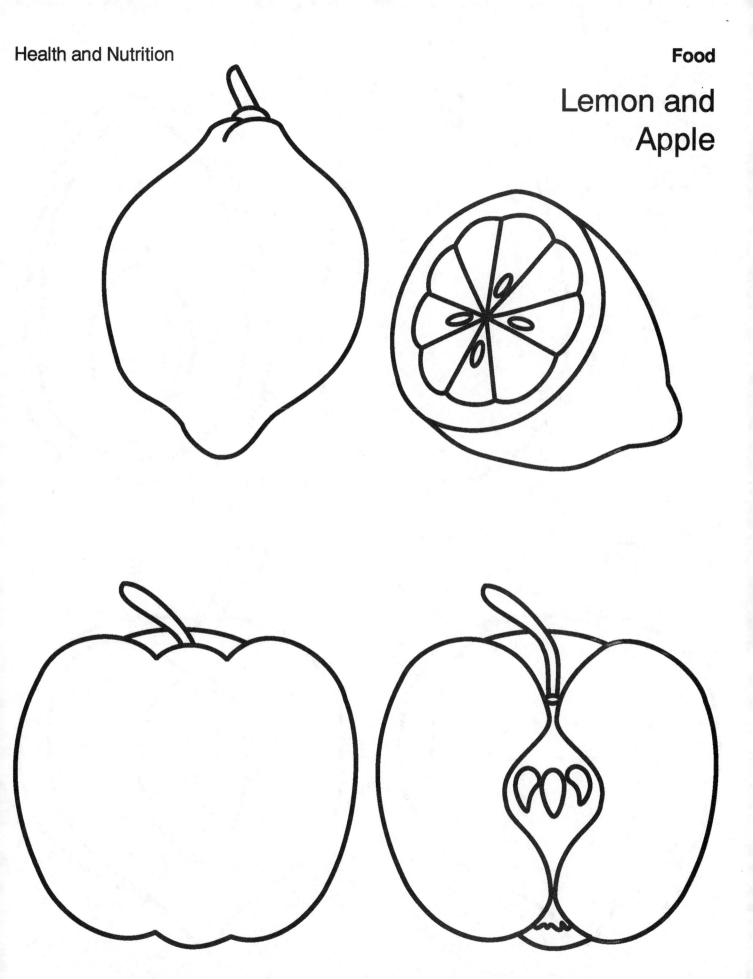

Avocado
and
Peach

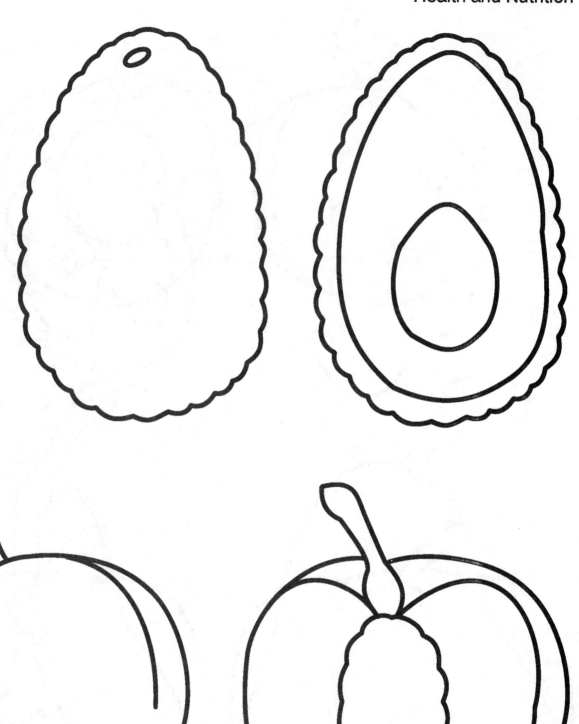

Apricot and Pear

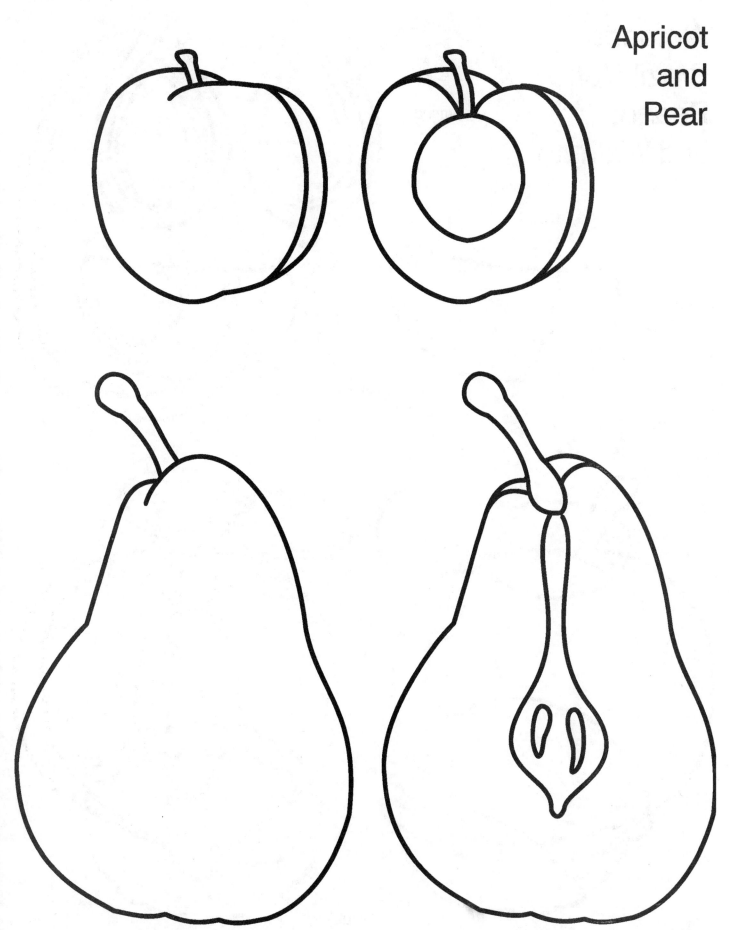

Almond,
Brazil Nut,
Peanut,
and Walnut

Almond

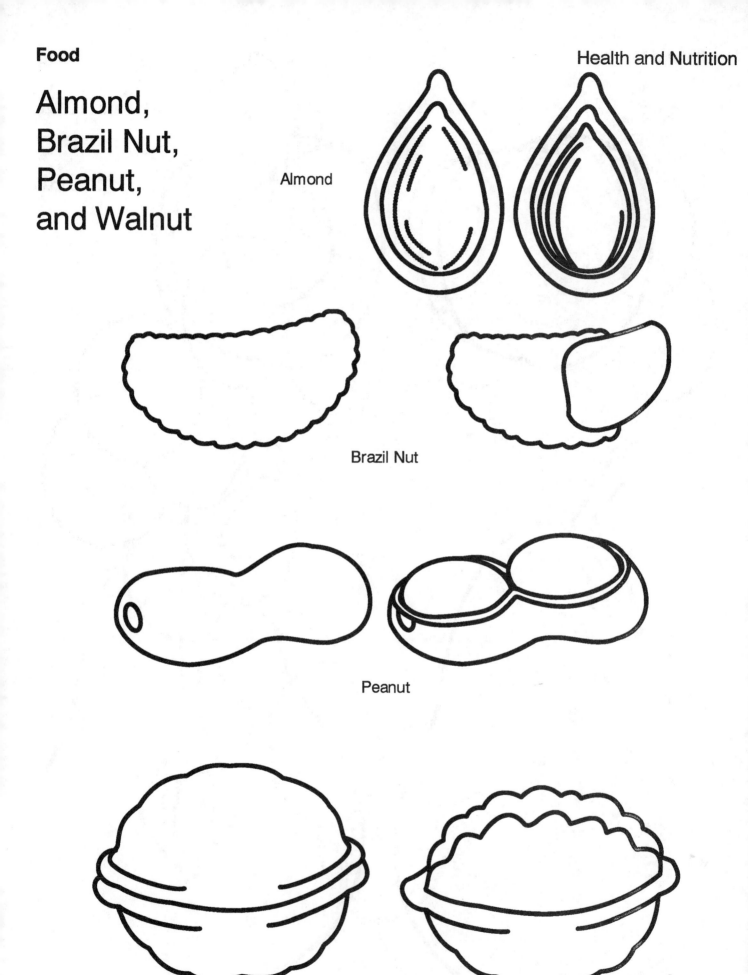

Brazil Nut

Peanut

Walnut

Grapes

Banana

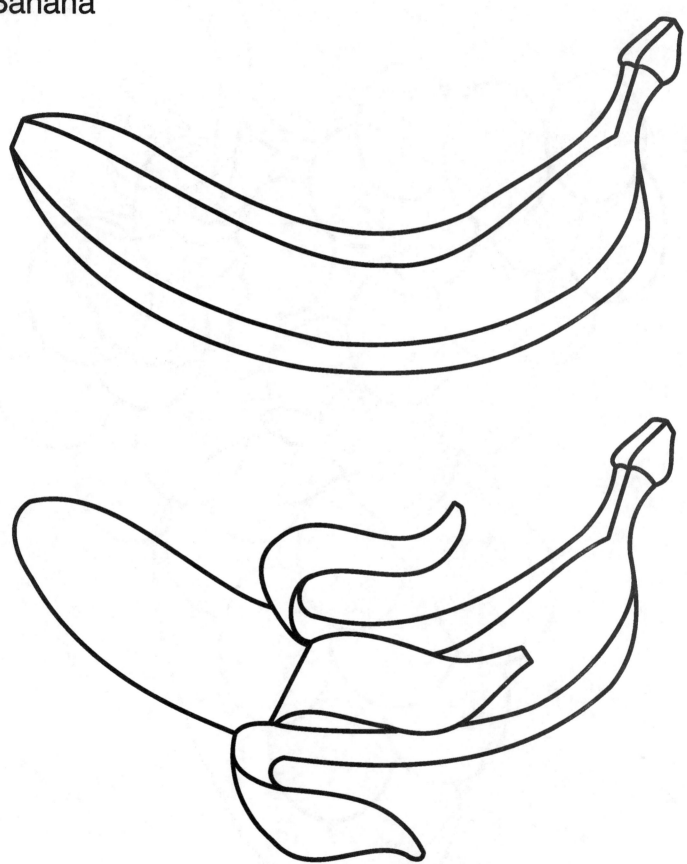

Berries

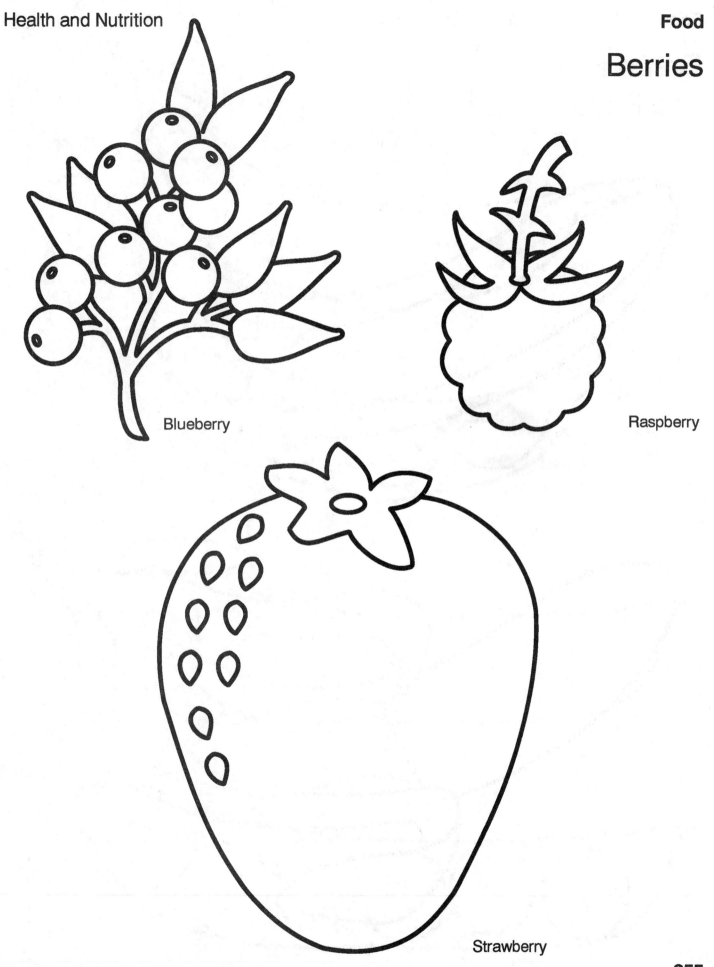

Blueberry

Raspberry

Strawberry

Green Beans and Peas

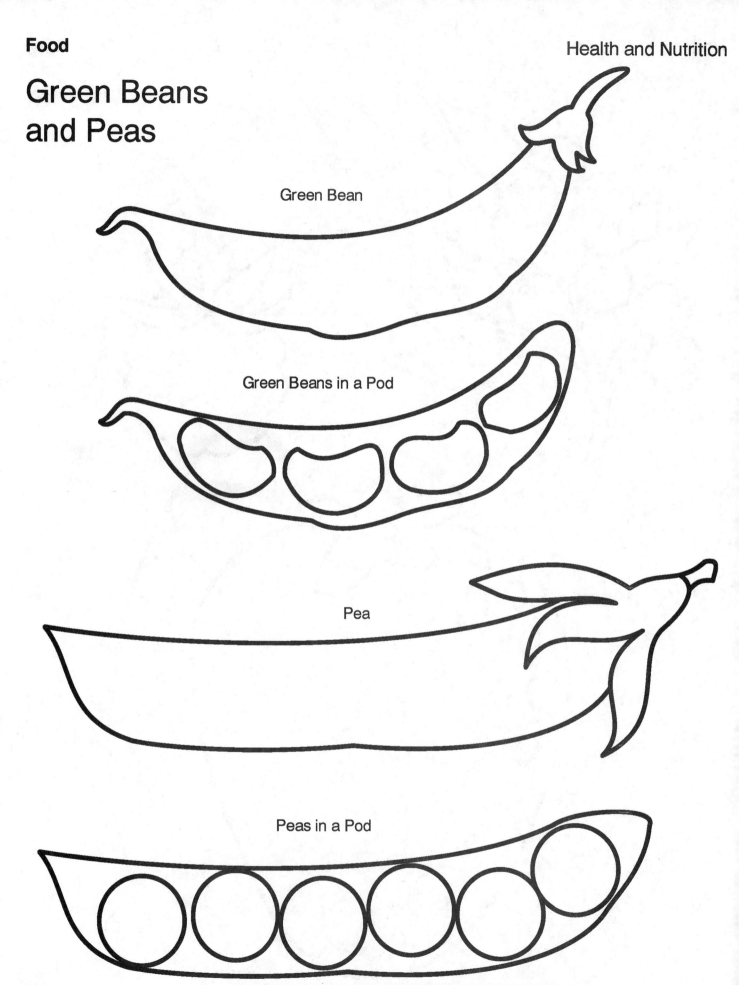

Green Bean

Green Beans in a Pod

Pea

Peas in a Pod

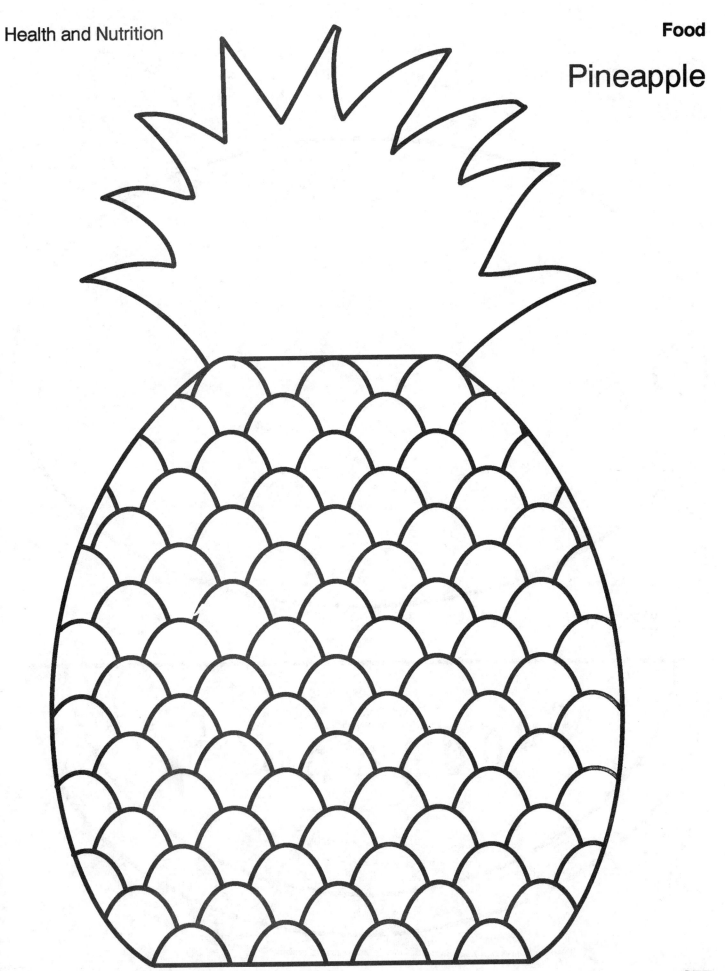

Watermelon

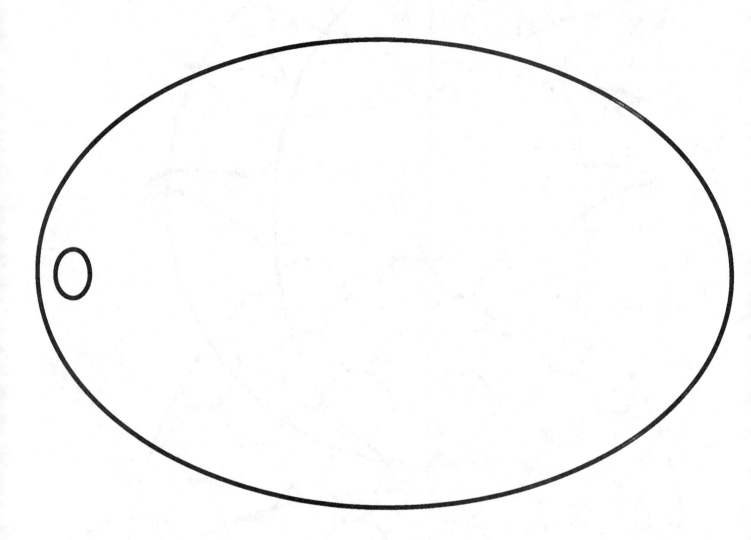

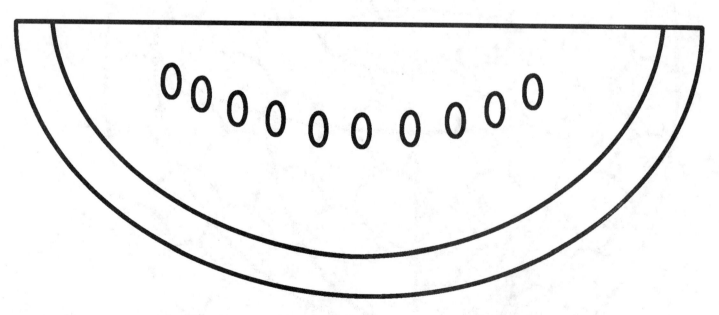

Cantaloupe

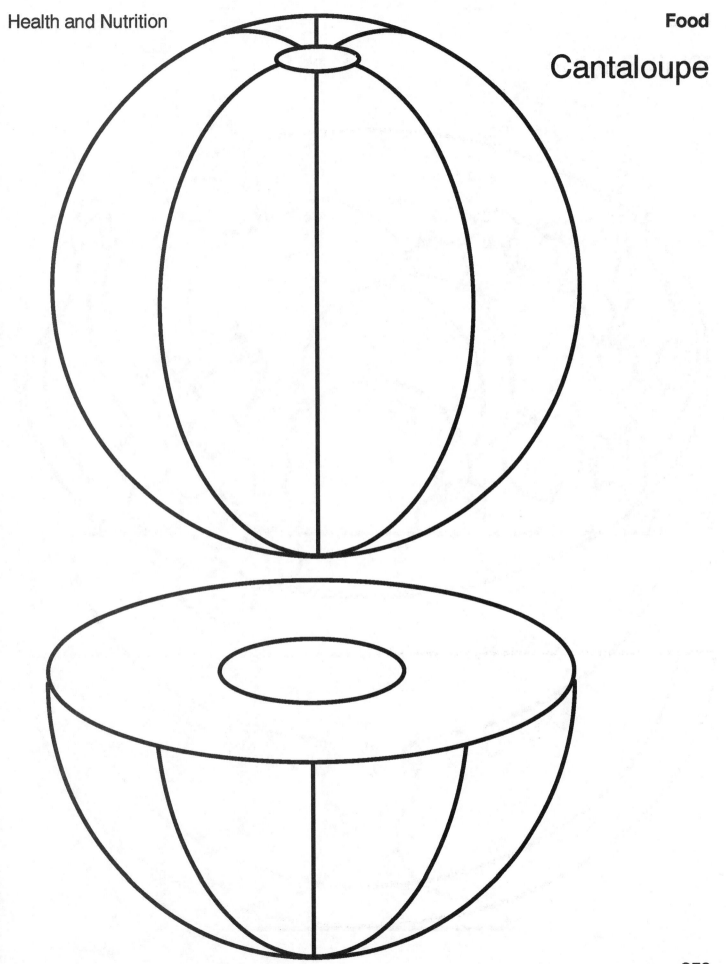

Fruit Bowl

Tomato
and Carrot

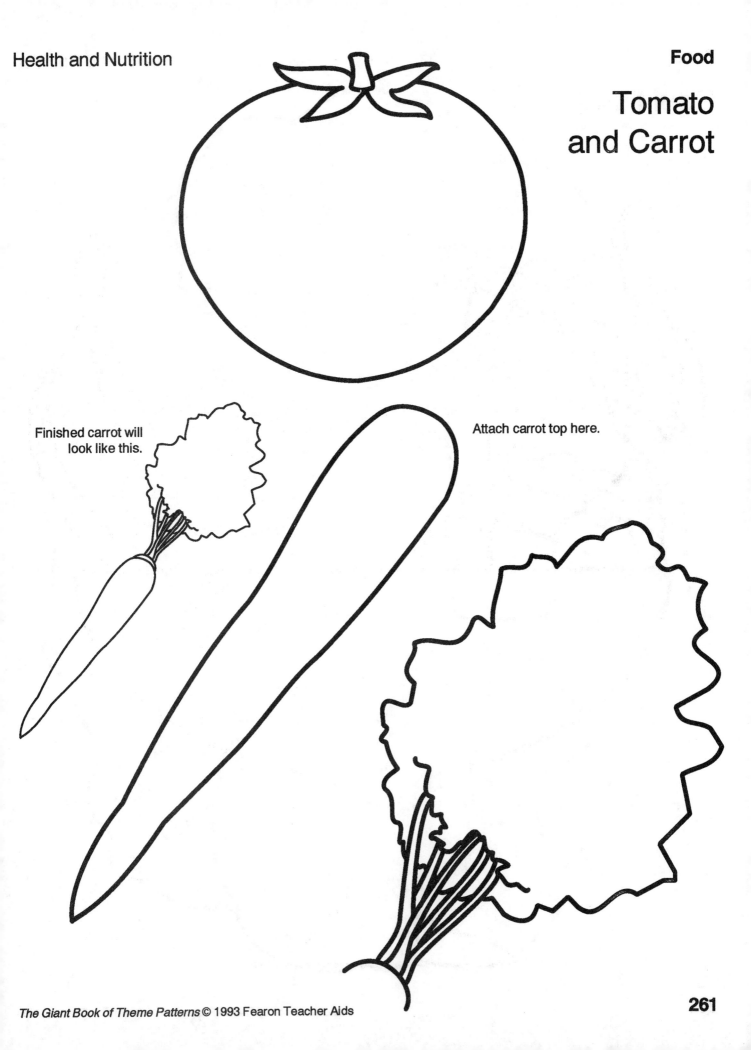

Finished carrot will
look like this.

Attach carrot top here.

Cauliflower

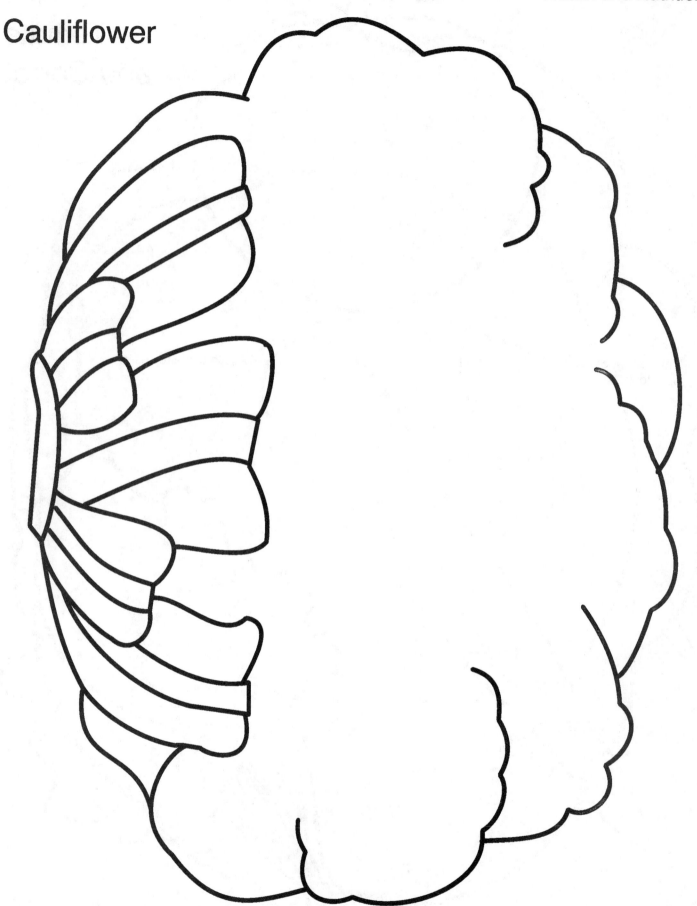

Lettuce

Zucchini and Broccoli

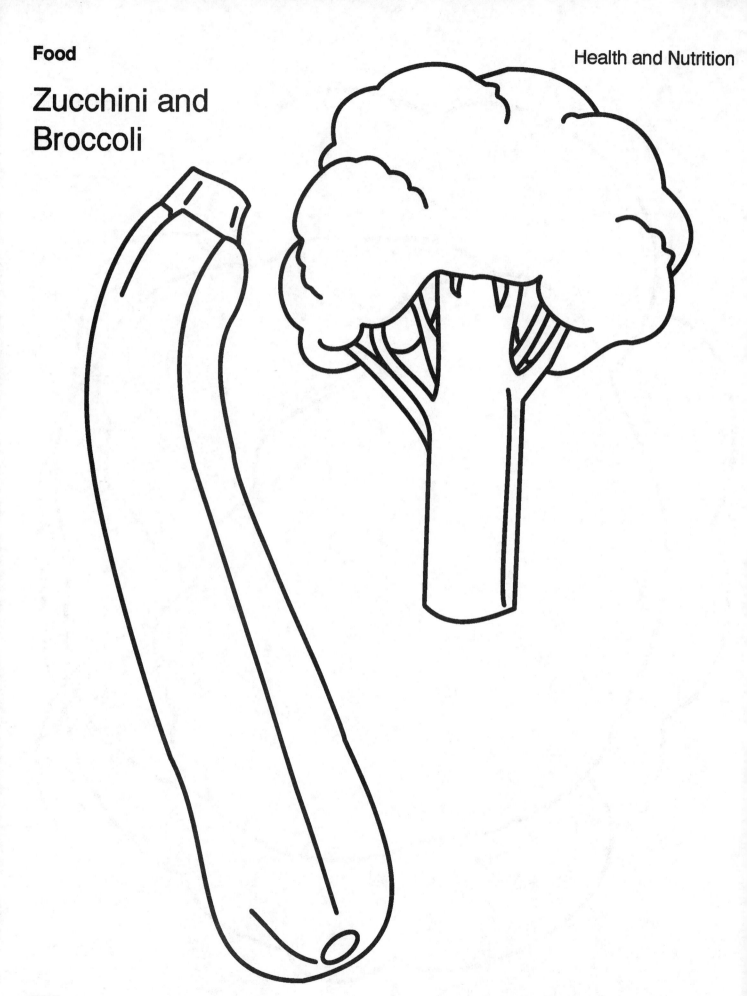

Onions and Garlic

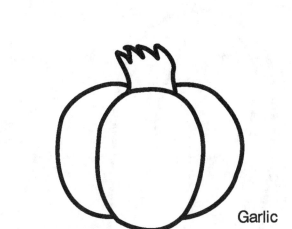

Garlic

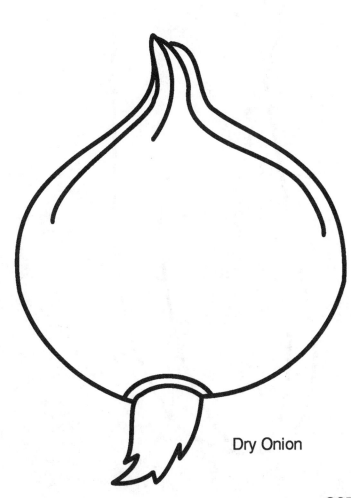

Dry Onion

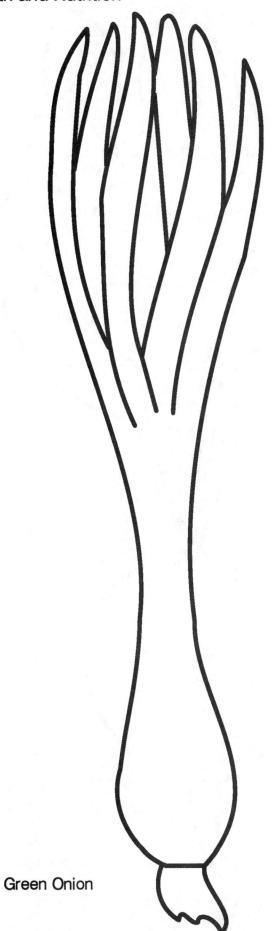

Green Onion

Beet and Cucumber

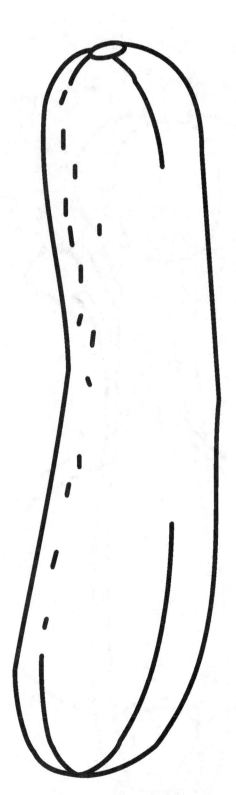

The Giant Book of Theme Patterns © 1993 Fearon Teacher Aids

Celery, Radish, and Bell Pepper

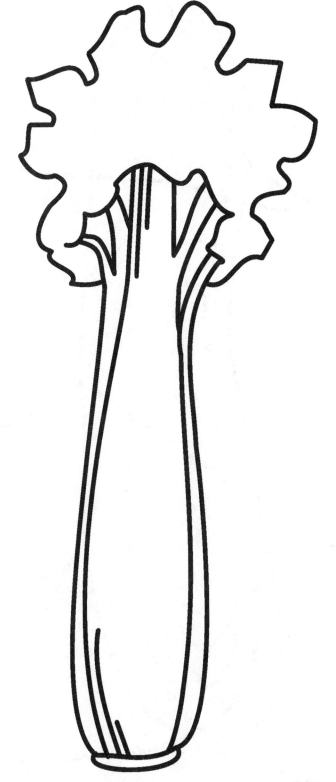

Yam and
Potato

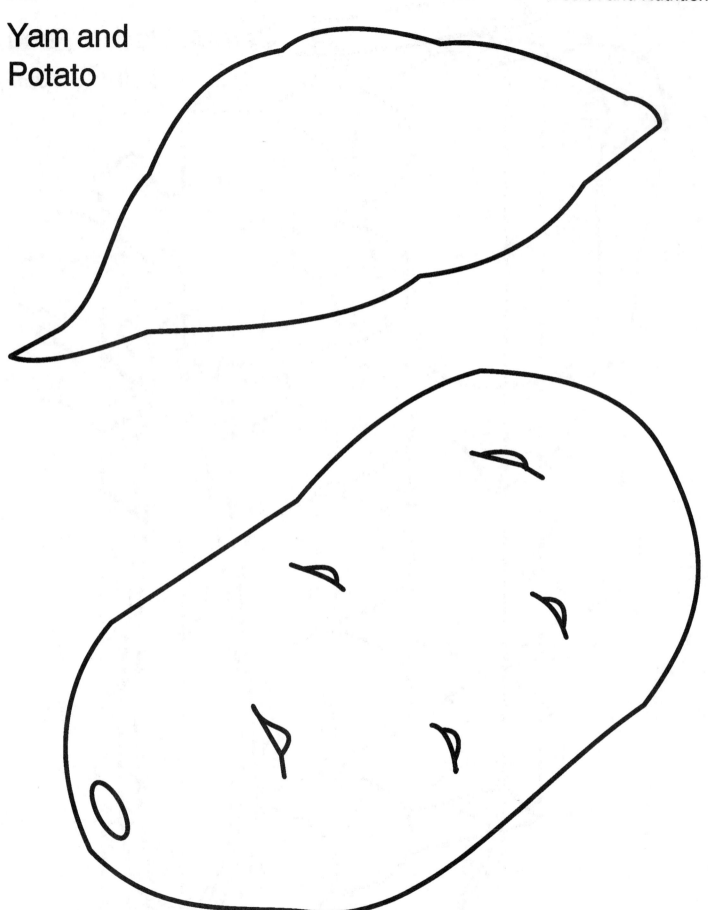

A Dozen Eggs
in a Carton

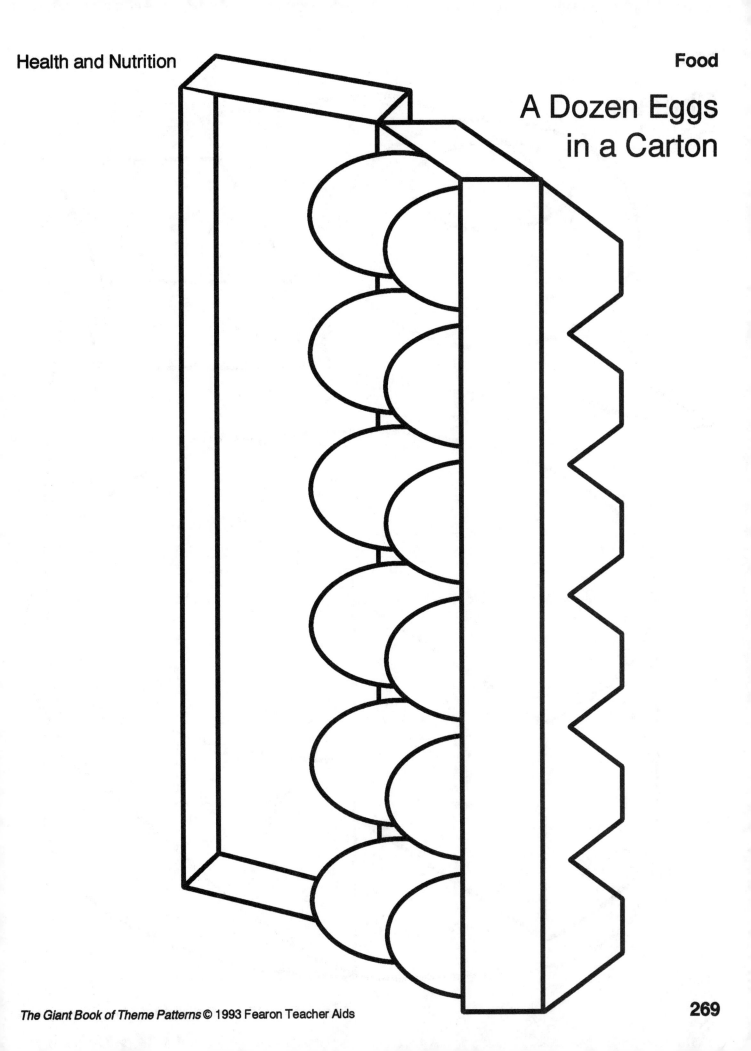

Cheese

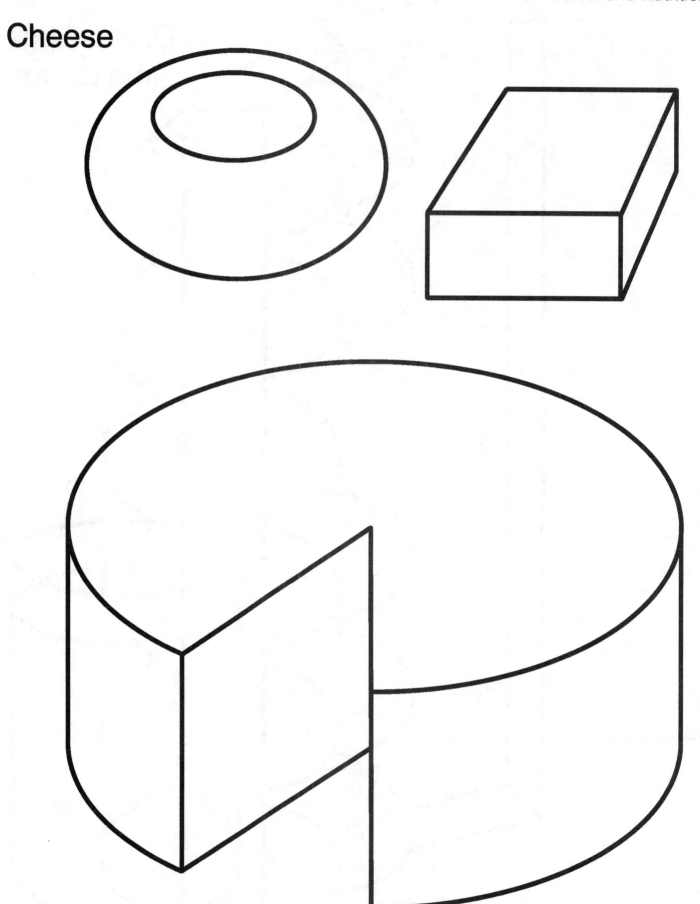

Milk

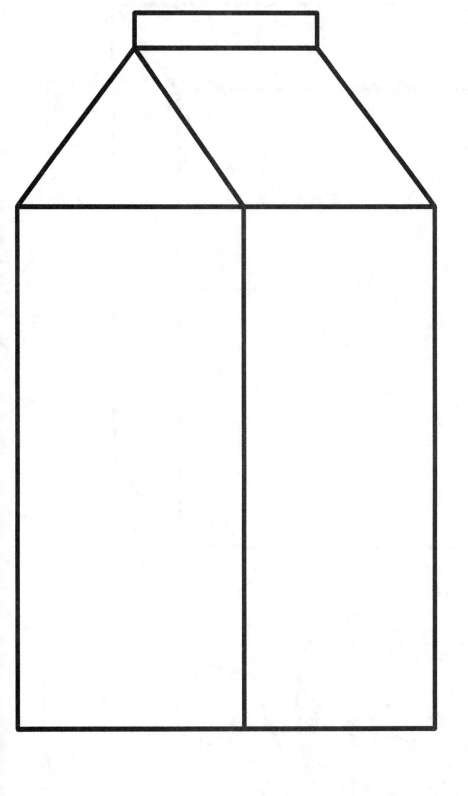

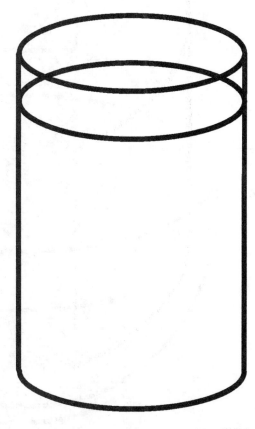

Box and Bowl
of Cereal

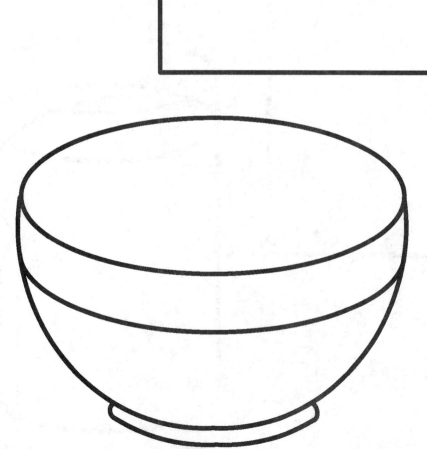

Bread

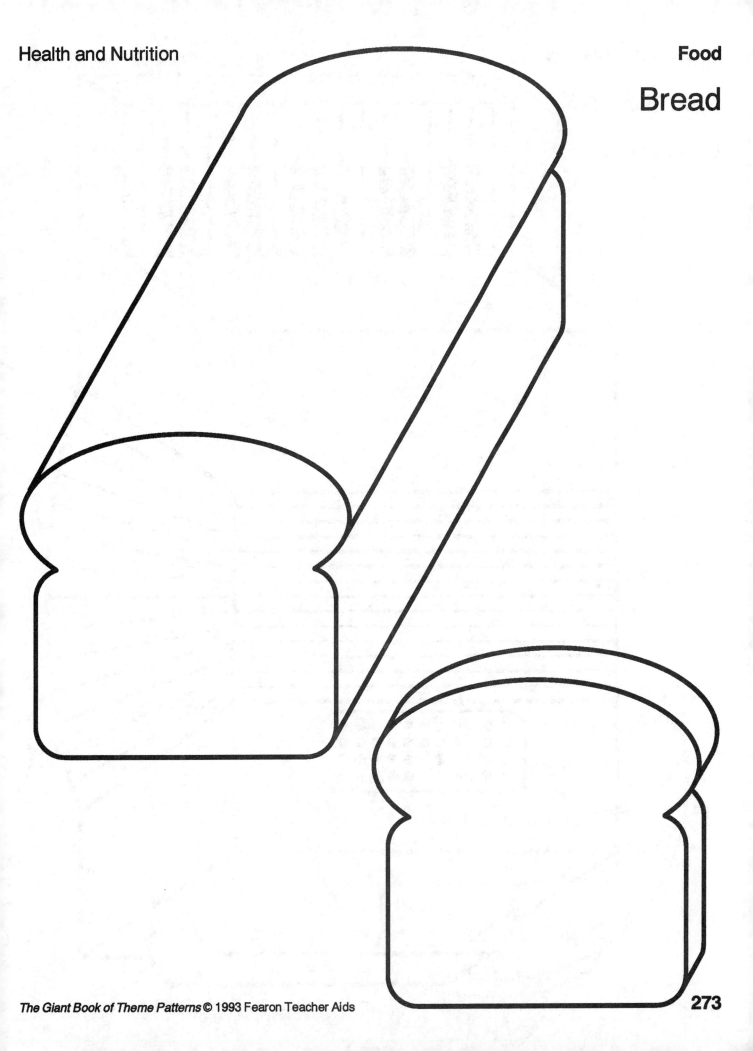

Accordion

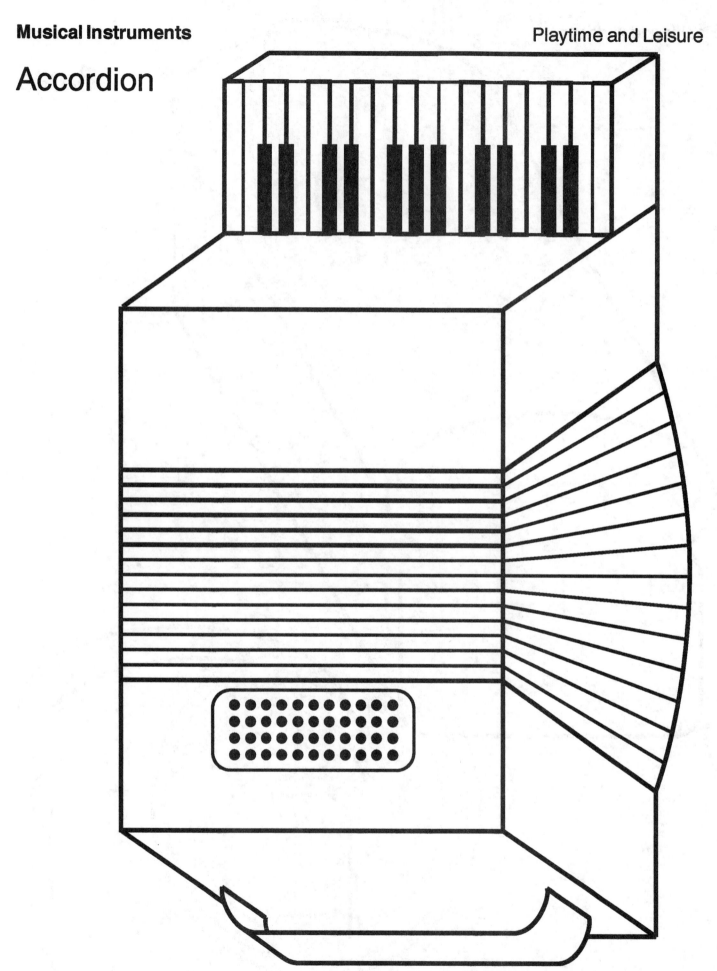

Banjo

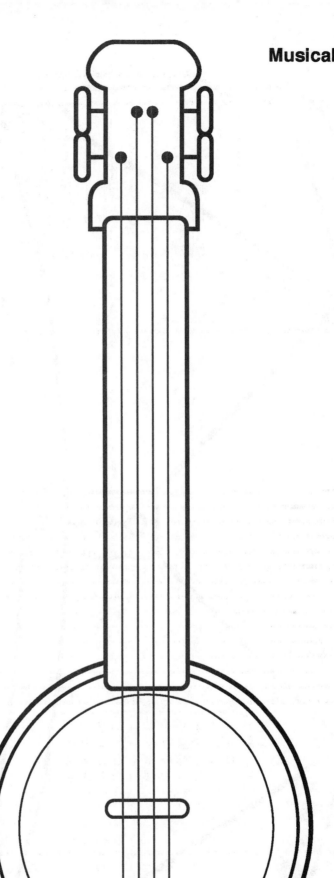

Drum

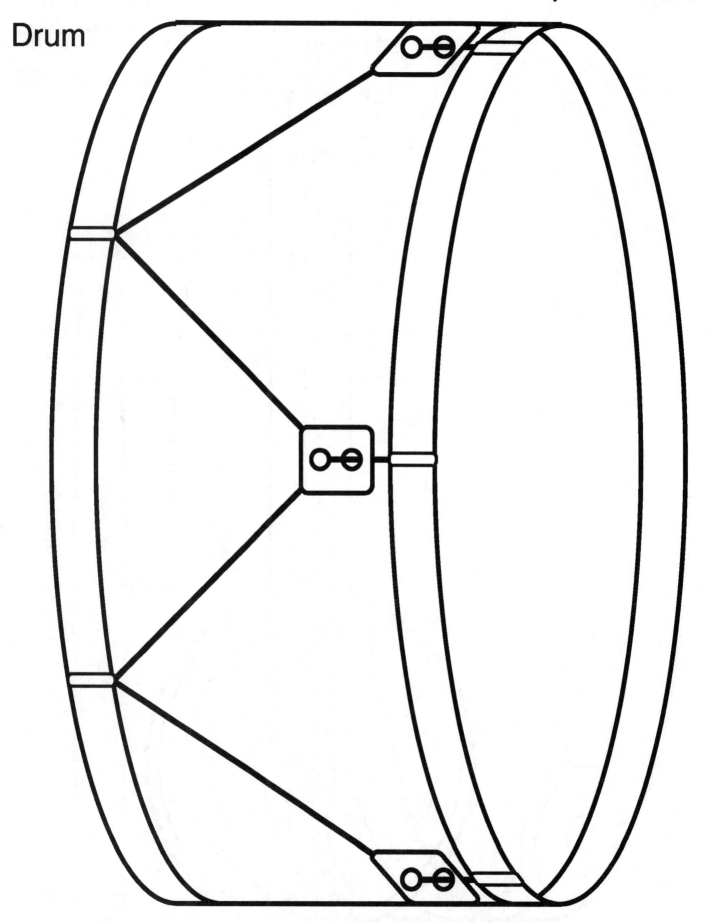

Tambourine and Drumstick

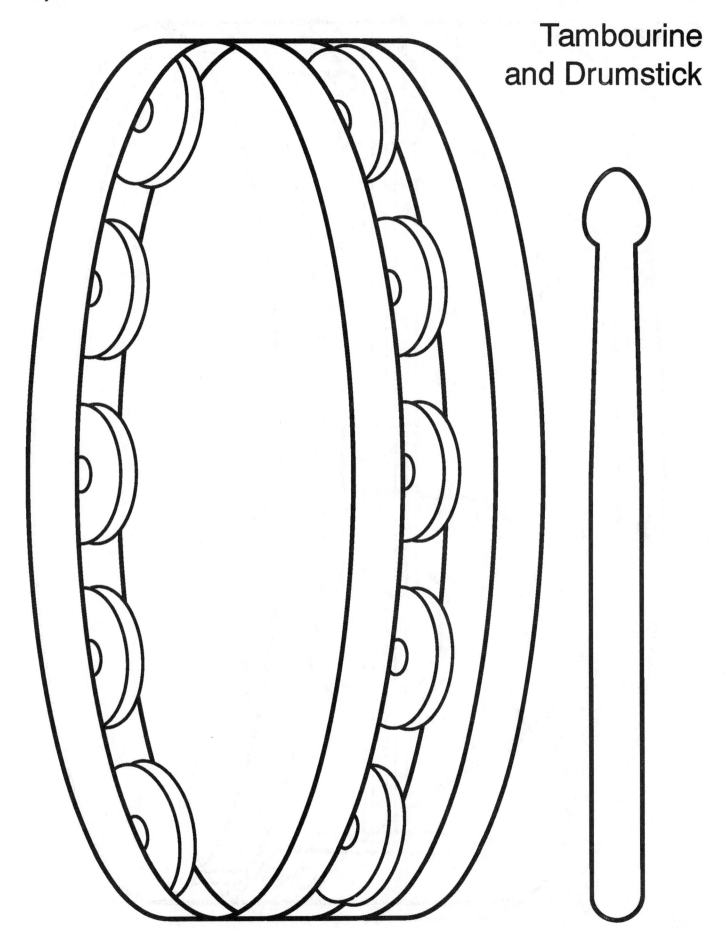

Guitar

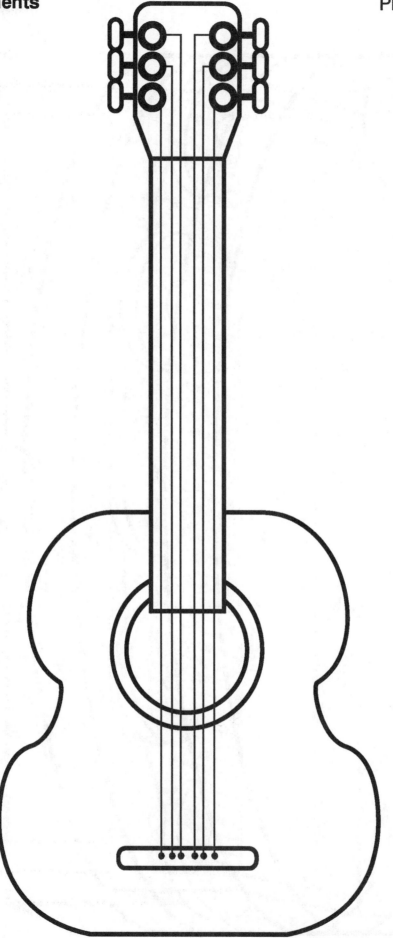

Piano

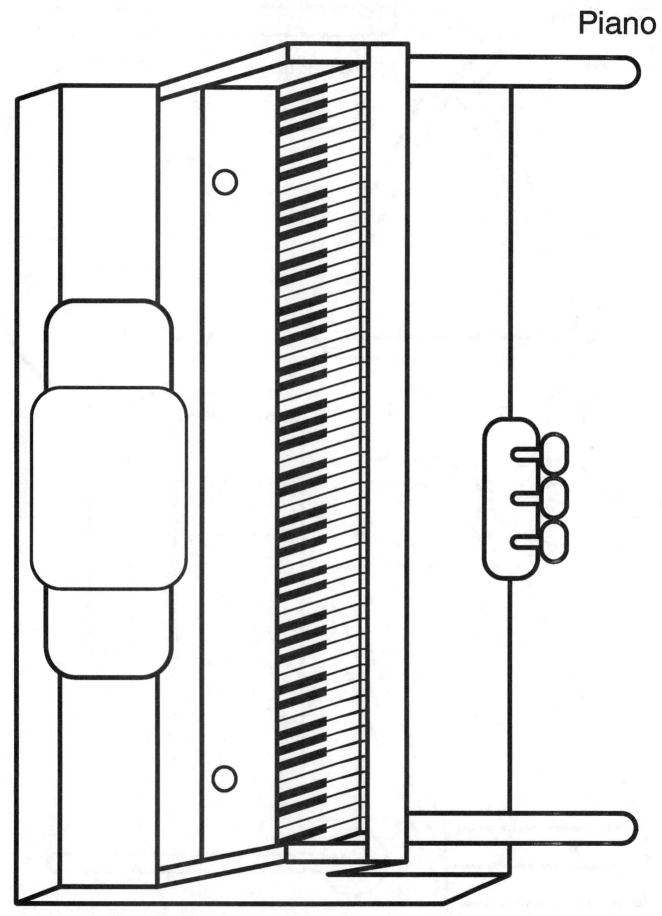

Rhythm
Band

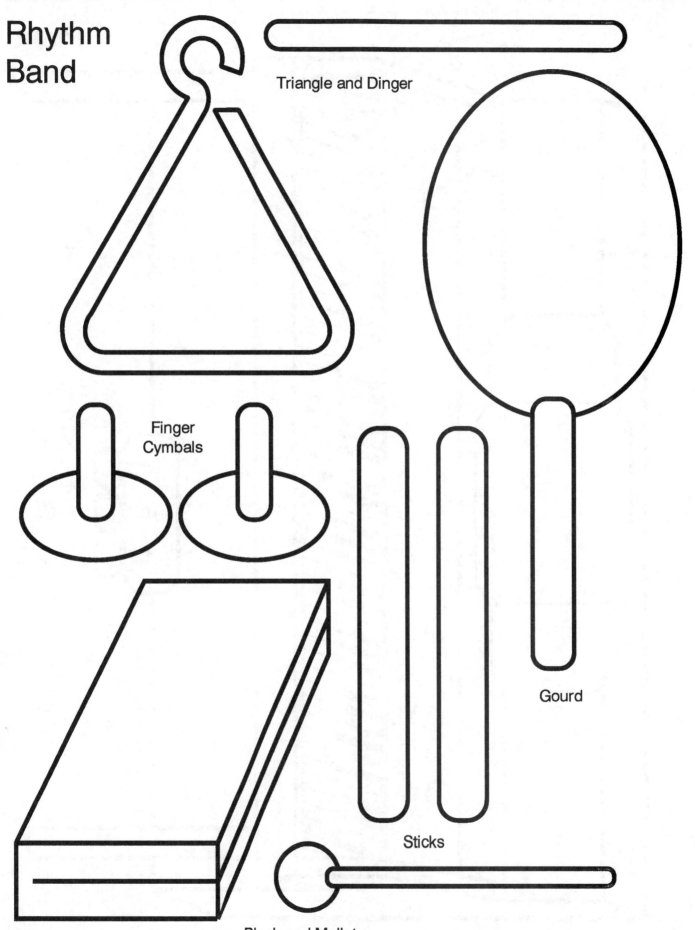

Triangle and Dinger

Finger
Cymbals

Gourd

Sticks

Block and Mallet

The Giant Book of Theme Patterns © 1993 Fearon Teacher Aids

Trumpet

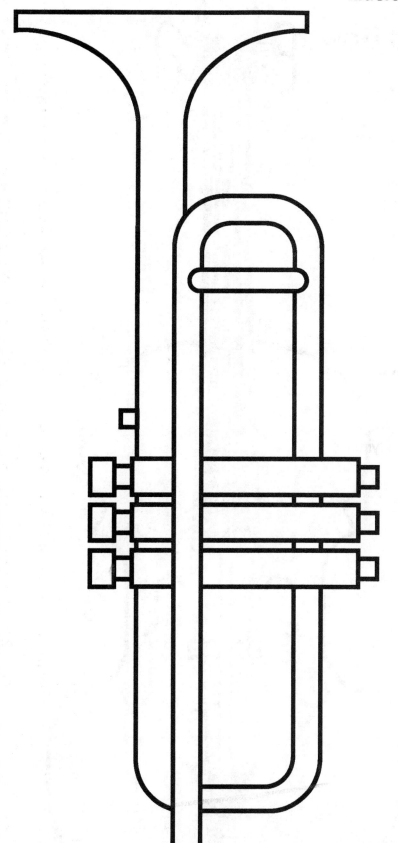

Violin and Bow

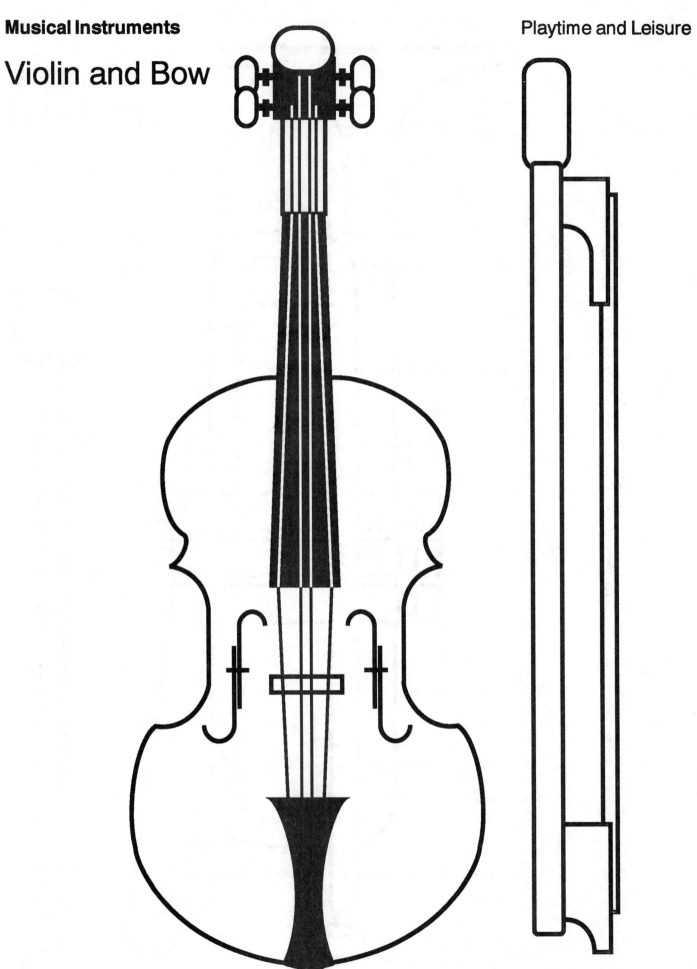

Xylophone
and Mallet

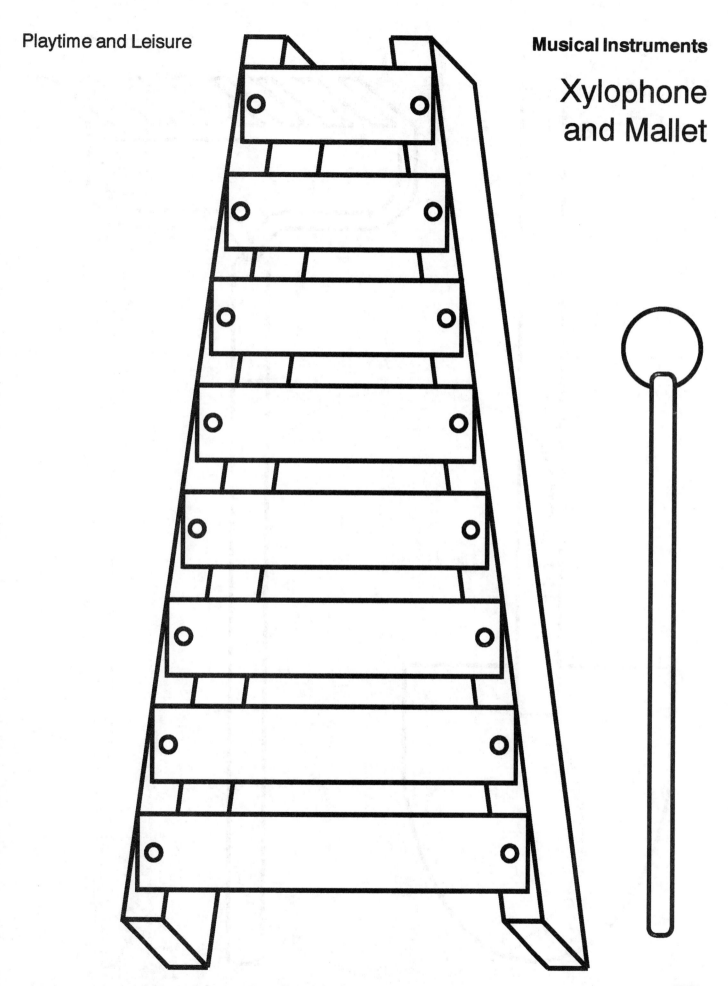

Shovel
and Rake

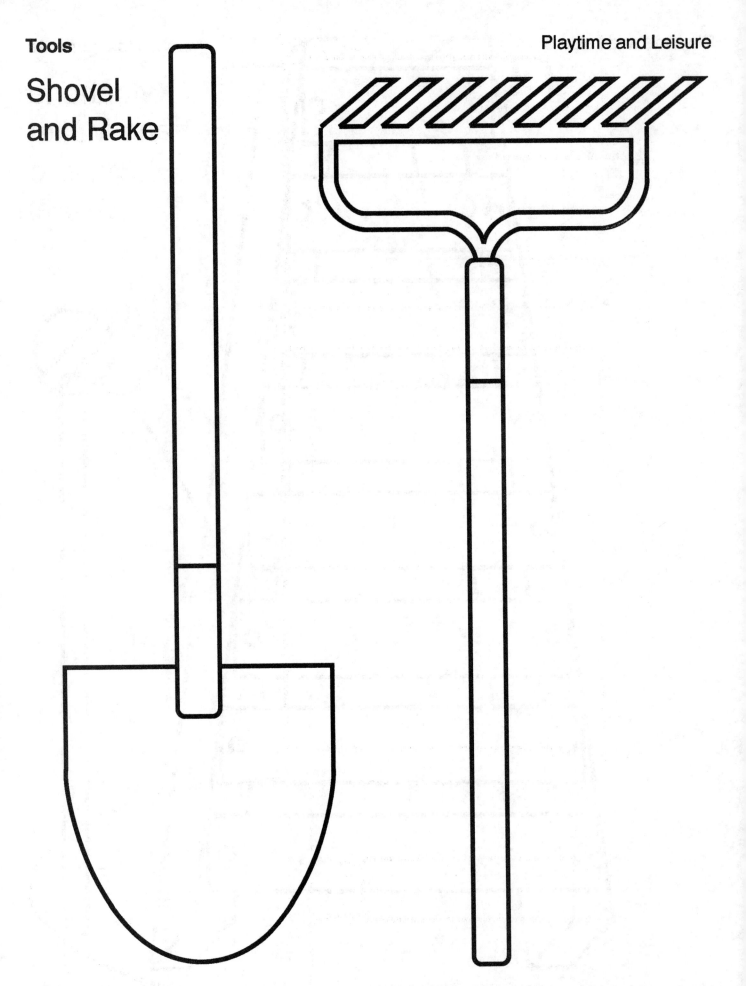

Watering Can, Glove, and Trowel

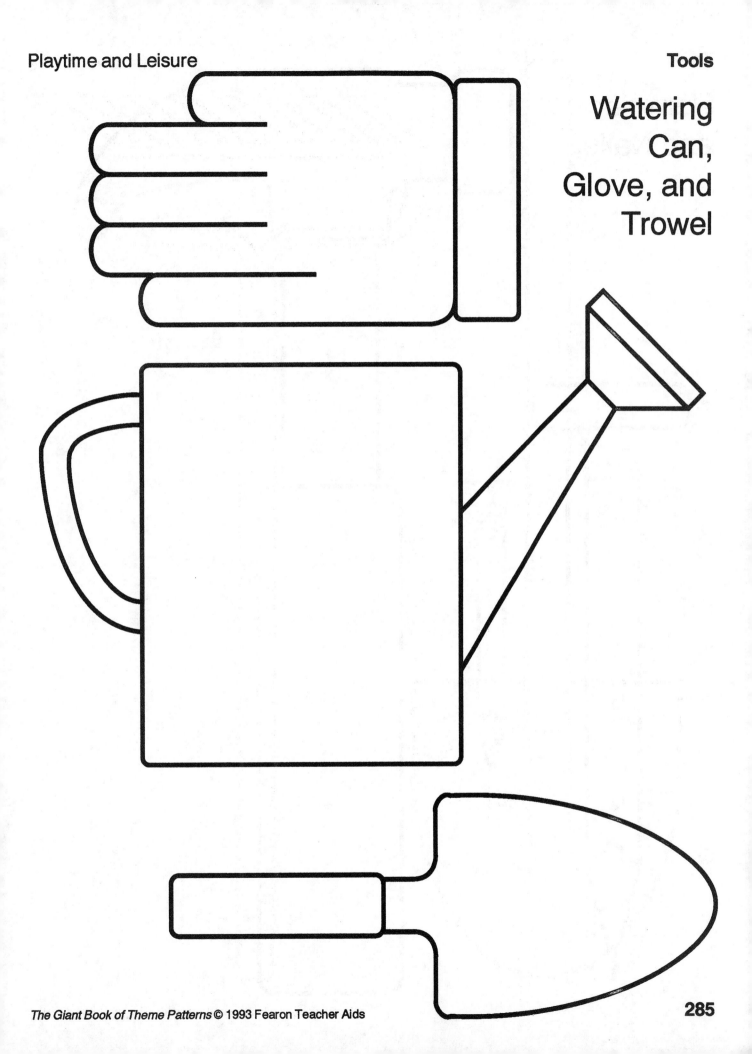

Hammer
and Nails

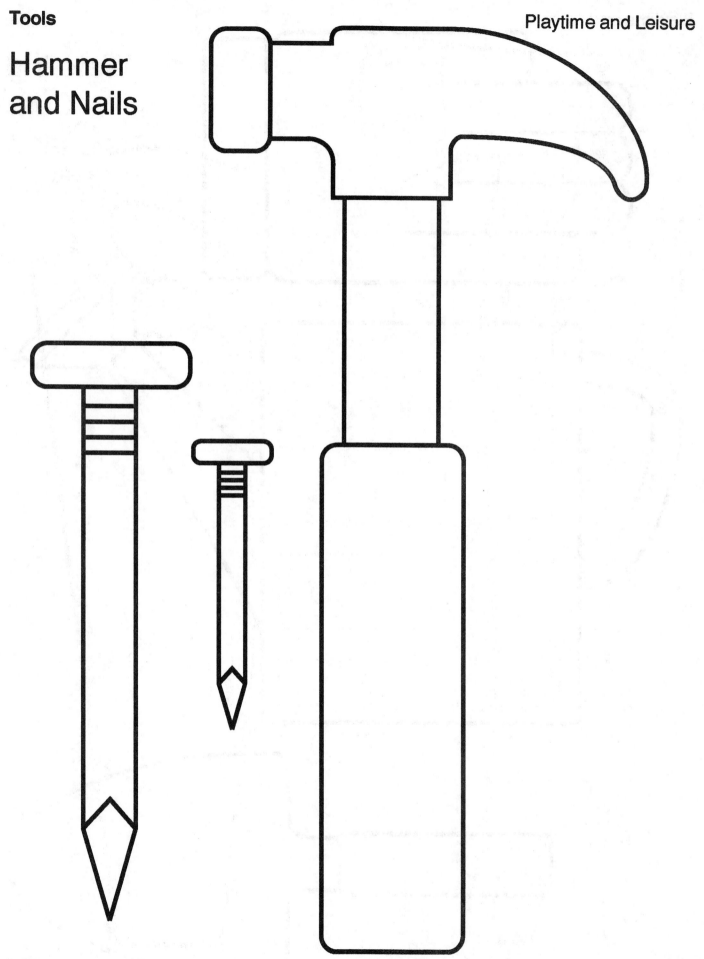

Saw and Ax

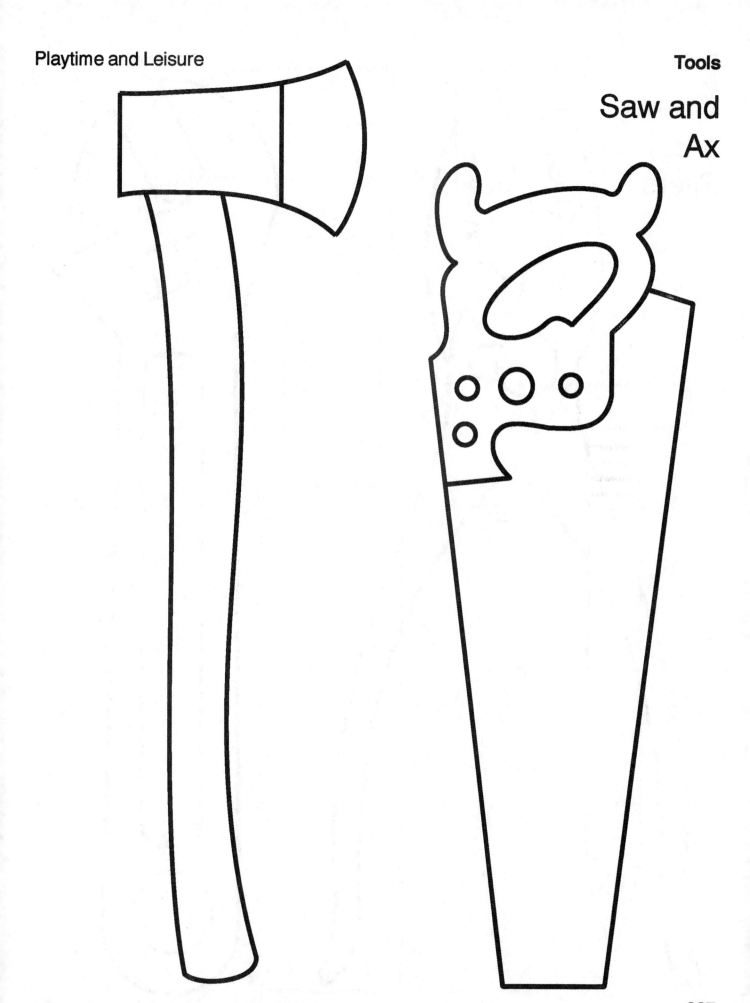

Wrench
and
Pliers

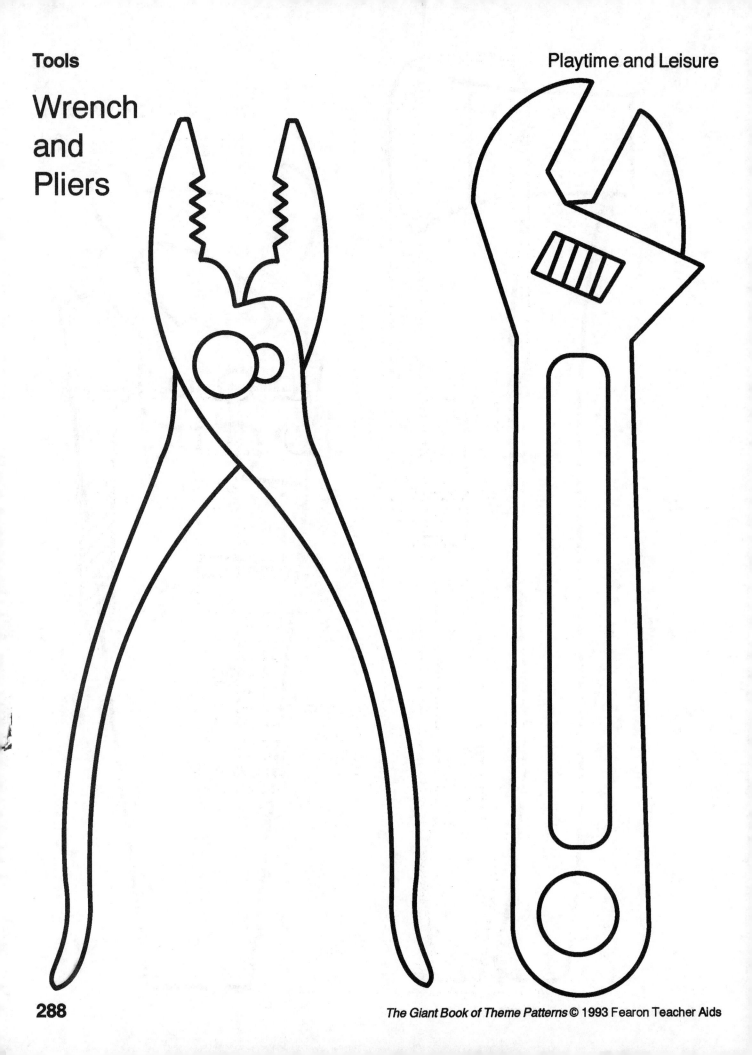

Doll

Teddy
Bear

Robot

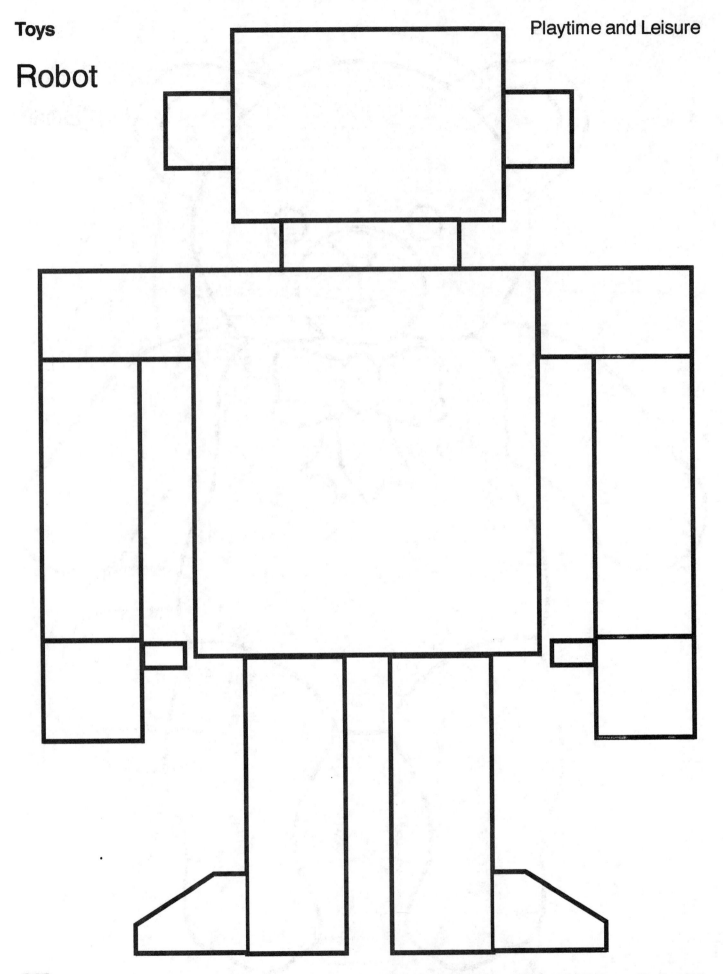

The Giant Book of Theme Patterns © 1993 Fearon Teacher Aids

Tennis Racket and Ball

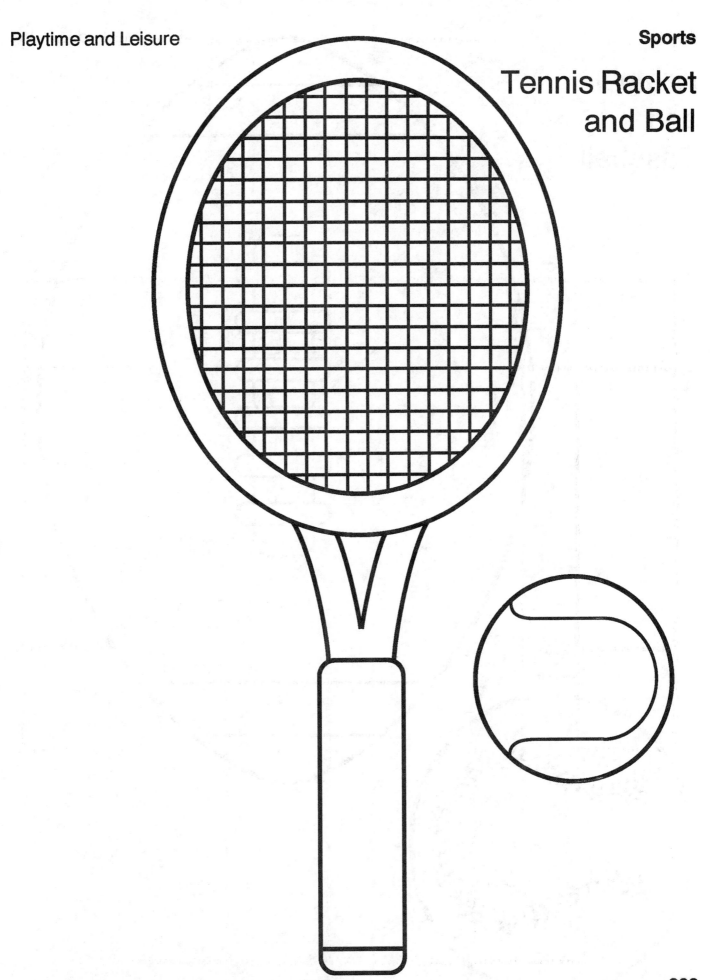

Football
and
Baseball

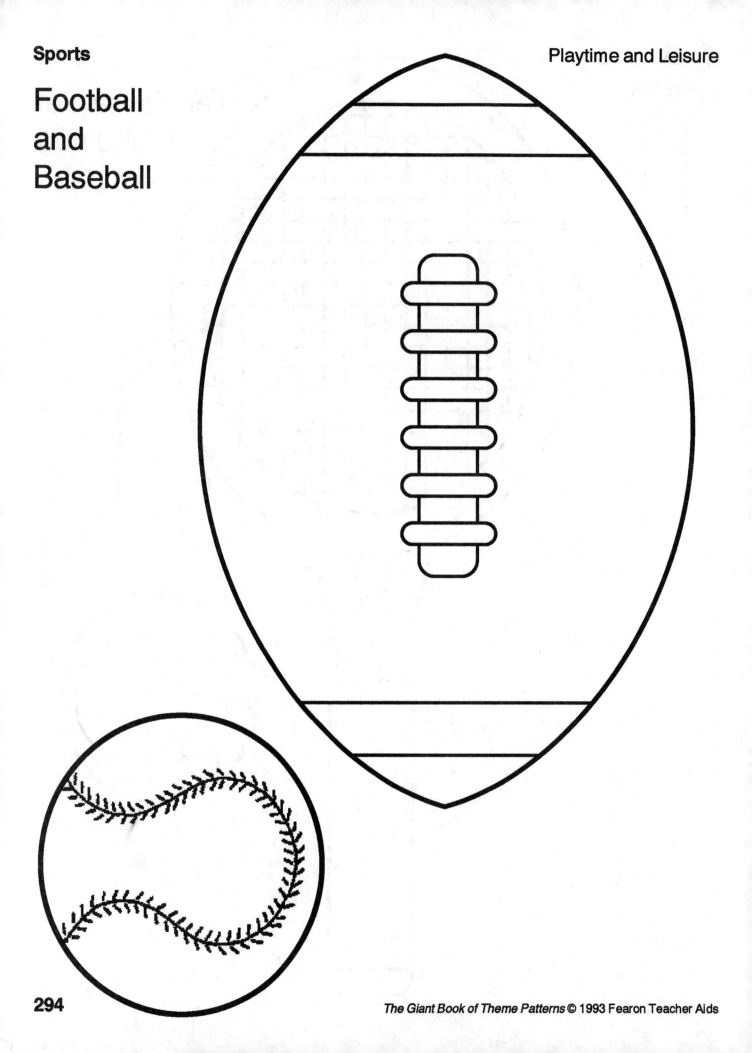

Baseball Bat
and
Soccer Ball

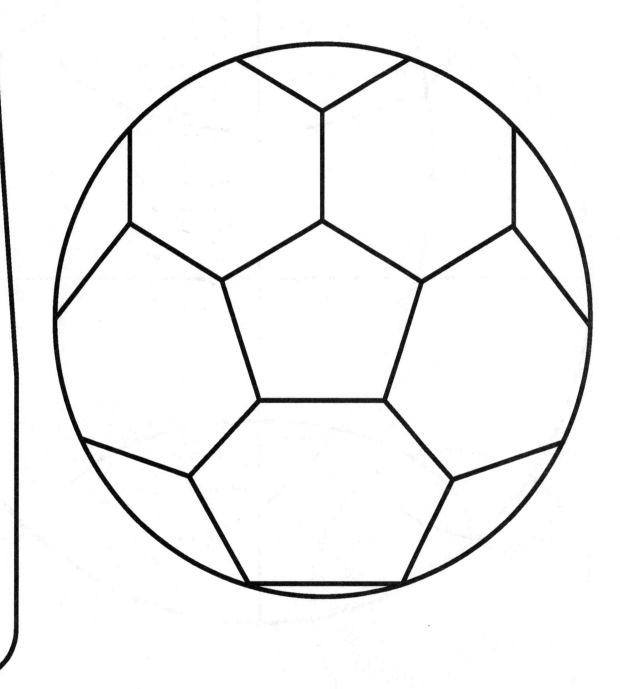

Basketball

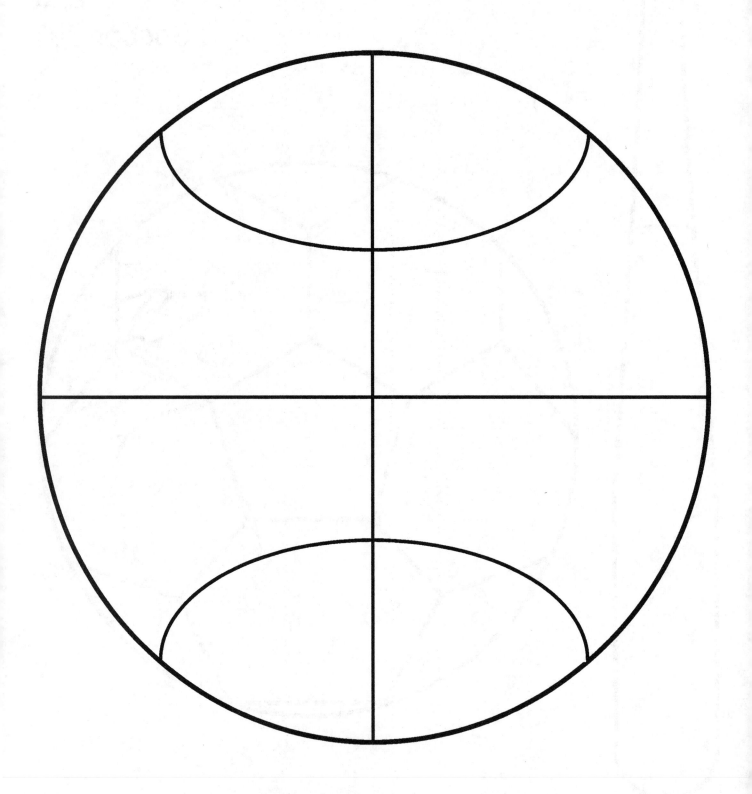

The Three Little Pigs

The Three Little Pigs' Houses

The Three Bears

The Three Billy Goats Gruff

Troll

Jack and
the Beanstalk

Little Red
Riding Hood

Big Bad Wolf

Wicked Witch

Princess

King

Gingerbread Person

Dragon

Unicorn

United States

Map of the States

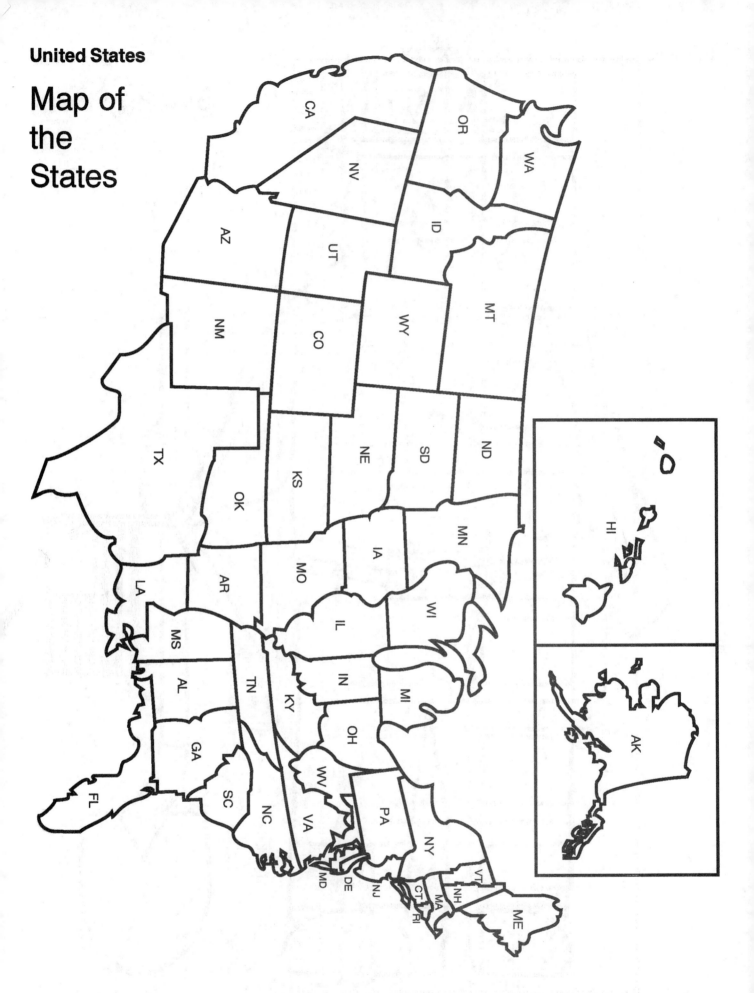

The White House

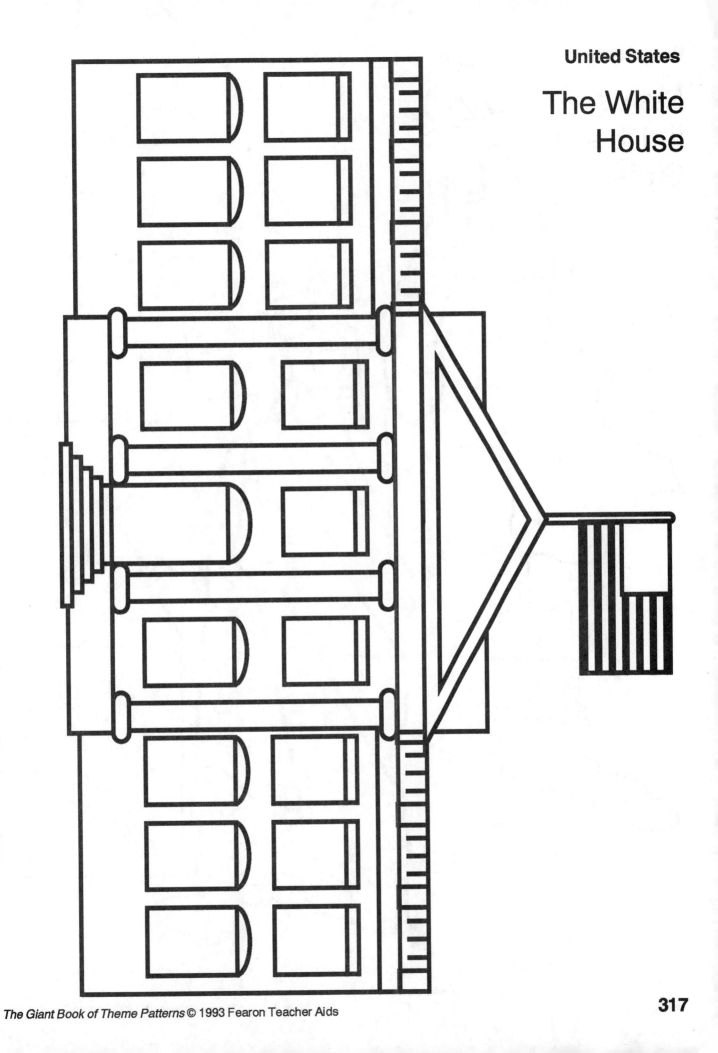

Statue
of Liberty

Globe

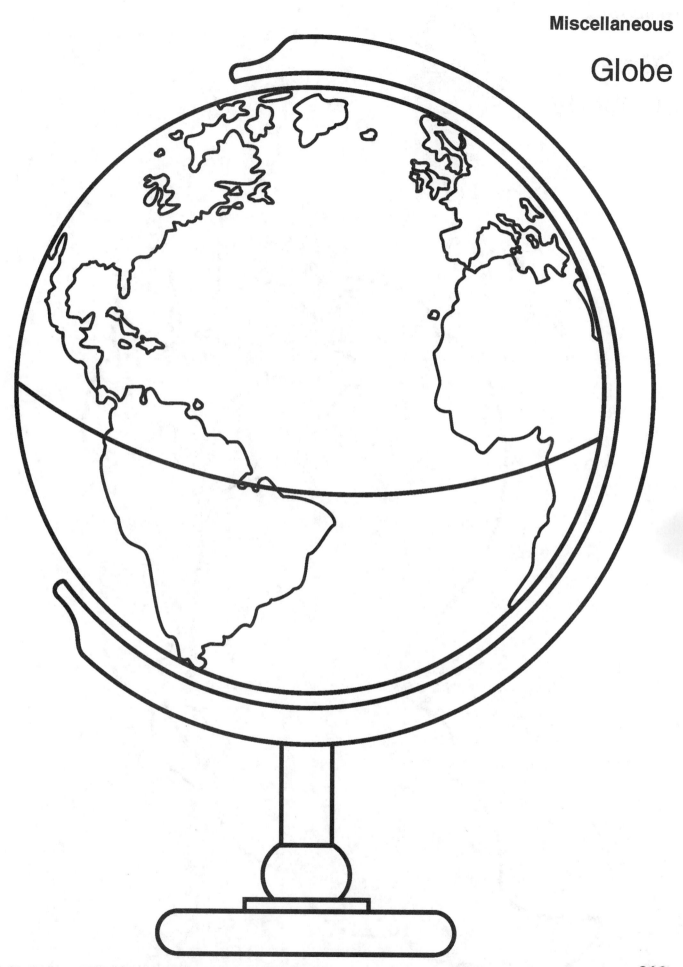

Wind

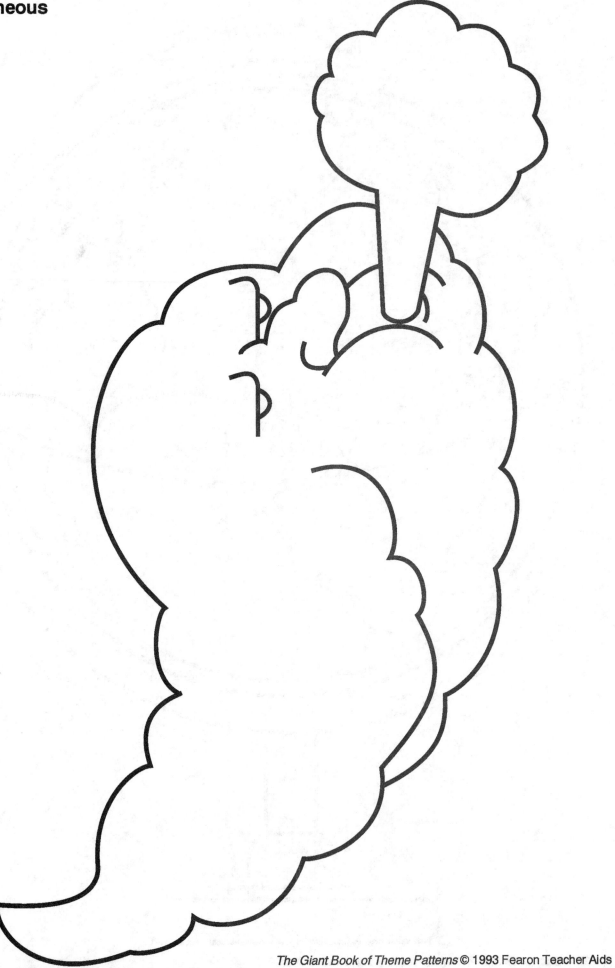

Fall Tree

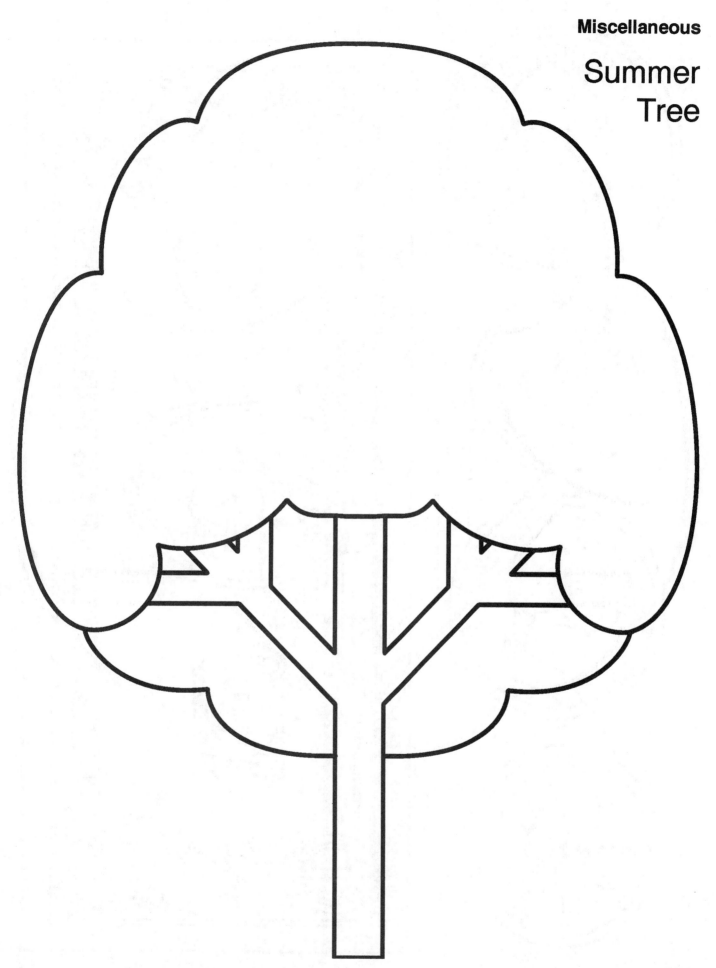

The Giant Book of Theme Patterns © 1993 Fearon Teacher Aids

ABCDEFG
HIJKLMNO
PQRSTUV
WXYZ!?",‚'

abcdefghijkl
mn opqrstuv
wxyz()&*+-
1234567890

Index